REALLY RIOTOUS SPORTS JOKES

REALLY RIOTOUS SPORTS JOKES

MICHAEL O'MARA BOOKS LTD

First published in Great Britain in 1999
by Michael O'Mara Books Limited
9 Lion Yard
Tremadoc Road
London SW4 7NQ

Copyright © Michael O'Mara Books Limited 1999

A CIP catalogue record for this book is available from the British Library

ISBN 1-85479-472-8

1 3 5 7 9 10 8 6 4 2

Cover design by Design 23

Designed and typeset by Design 23

Printed and bound by WSOY, Finland

FANTASY FOOTBALL

Des Lynam, Alan Hansen and Andy Gray are standing before God at the throne of Heaven. God looks at the three of them and says 'Before granting you a place at my side, I must first ask you what you believe in.' Addressing Alan Hansen first he asks 'What do you believe?'

Big Al looks God in the eye and says 'I believe football to be the food of life. Nothing else brings so much joy to so many people from the slums of Sao Paolo, to the mansions of Chelsea. I have devoted my whole life to bring such joy to the people who stood on the terraces at Anfield.' God looks at Alan, and offers him the seat to his left. He then turns to Andy Gray. 'And you Mr. Gray, what do you believe?'

Andy stands up and passionately declares 'I believe that courage, honour and passion are the fundamentals of life, and I've spent my whole playing career providing a living embodiment of these traits.' God, moved by the passion of Andy Gray's speech, offers him the seat to his right.

Finally he turns to Des. 'And what about you, Mr. Lynam, what do you believe in?' 'I believe' replies Des very smoothly, 'that you are in my seat.'

A couple are in the middle of a very messy divorce, and find themselves in court battling over the custody of their only child. In order to make a fair decision, the judge takes the young boy into his private chambers, so that he can ask him who he'd prefer to live with, whilst his parents are not around.

'Would you like to live with your mother?' enquires the judge. 'No' replies the boy 'she hits me.'

'Would you like to live with your father?' the judge asks. But the boy replies 'No, he hits me too.'

'Well, who would you like to live with?' asks the judge. 'I'd like to live with Nottingham Forest football club' the boy replies. 'Why on earth would you want to live with Nottingham Forest football club?' asks the surprised judge. 'Because they never beat anyone' the boy replies.

A footballer with a bit of a reputation as a prima donna is on a long-haul flight when he desperately needs the loo, but there is a huge queue of people in front of him. He isn't averse to taking advantage of his celebrity status so he immediately starts throwing a tantrum.

The stewardess is fed up of having stroppy sports stars on her flights and she doesn't want to upset any of the other passengers by letting him barge in at the front of the queue. So she takes him to the staff ladies loo where there is no queue. However, she warns him that he must not press any of the buttons.

Whilst the footballer is sat there, he spies the four buttons in front of him, and curiosity gets the better of him. After all, he is a celebrity, he can do what he likes. There are four buttons, one marked WW, one marked WA, the next is marked PP and the fourth is marked ATR. So the footballer presses the one marked WW, and a jet of warm water sprays gently onto his arse. This is quite pleasurable, so he presses the next one, marked WA, and warm air dries his arse.

'Wow!' he exclaims. 'The girls have a really easy time of things.' Next he presses the button marked PP and a powder puff appears and applies scented powder to his behind. Well, after that he can't wait to see what the fourth button will do, so he eagerly presses the button marked ATR. However on pressing it he's suddenly knocked unconscious.

When the footballer wakes up, he discovers that he's in hospital. He hasn't a clue what's happened to him, so in his usual rude manner he demands to see a nurse immediately, to explain what has happened. 'The stewardess told you not to touch any of the buttons' explained the nurse 'and you deliberately ignored her by pressing the one marked ATR.'

'So what' replied the cocky footballer. 'What does ATR stand for anyway?'

'Automatic tampon remover' replied the nurse. 'You'll find your penis under your pillow.'

Quasimodo asked Esmerelda if he really was the ugliest man alive. Esmerelda said 'Go upstairs and ask the magic mirror who is the ugliest man alive, and the mirror will give you the correct answer.' Five minutes later Quasimodo came back down the stairs looking very pleased with himself and asked Esmerelda 'Who on earth is Iain Dowie?'

Two teenage boys were playing football in the park in Manchester when one of them was attacked by a rotweiler. Thinking quickly, the other lad grabbed a huge plank of wood which he then forced into the dog's collar, twisting it hard, so that the dog's neck was broken and he died.

Whilst this was going on a local newspaper reporter was watching the whole event, and thought that the young lad's bravery would make a brilliant cover story for the next edition. He rushed over to the two boys and frantically began scribbling, 'Manchester City fan saves friend's life.'

'Hang on a minute' said the boy 'I don't support Manchester City.' So the reporter crossed out 'City' and wrote 'United' instead. 'I'm not a United fan either' the boy protested. The reporter turned to the boy and enquired 'Well just who do you support?' 'Liverpool' the lad replied.

The reporter let out a heavy sigh, before ripping out the page and writing on a clean page 'Scouse bastard kills family pet.'

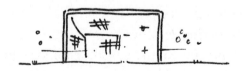

An old Palestinian retired to Ireland to escape his home country's violence. He bought a little cottage in a tiny village, where there was only one shop. This shop served as the pub, the post office, the greengrocer, the undertaker and the lawyer.

About a year later the old man died, and his son flew over to Ireland to arrange his father's burial. He went into the shop to speak to the undertaker and said to the undertaker 'I would like to see my father one last time before he is buried, so that I can say goodbye.' The coffin was opened, and the son was outraged to see that his father had been placed in the coffin wearing a Middlesbrough football club shirt. 'What is the meaning of this?' he shouted to him: 'My father hated football all of his life, and you've put him into a football shirt for all eternity.'

'I don't understand' replied the bewildered undertaker. 'I drew up your father's last will for him and it specifically states that he wishes to be buried in a Middlesbrough shirt'. The son didn't believe that his father would have requested that for one moment, so he asked to see the will. The undertaker went behind the bar, rummaged through a pile of papers and pulled out the will. 'See' he cried triumphantly. 'Here it is in black and white; I wish to be buried in the Gazza strip.'

Paddy is appearing on 'Who Wants to be a Millionaire'.

Chris Tarrant: 'Paddy, you've done very well so far. £64, 000 and one life left which is phone a friend. The next question will give you £125,000 if you get it right but if you get it wrong you will be out of the game and will go away with £32,000. Are you ready?'

Paddy: 'Sure I am Chris.'

Chris: 'On the screen is a photo of a current Manchester United player as a baby. Which Manchester United player is it? – Now think about this carefully Paddy, it's worth £125,000, meaning that you are only three questions away from £1million.'

Paddy: 'I think I know who it is, but I'm not 100% sure. No I'm sure it's Beckham, but can I phone a friend Chris, just to check?'

Chris: 'Yes Paddy. Who do you want to phone?'

Paddy: 'I'll phone Mick.'

Mick: 'Hello?'

Chris: 'Hello Mick. It's Chris Tarrant here from 'Who wants to be a Millionaire' – I have Paddy O'Shea here and he is doing really well. He's already won £64,000, but needs your help to get to £125,000. Mick are you next to a fax machine? - This is a visual question I'm faxing you. The next voice you here will be Paddy's – he'll explain the question and you have 30 seconds to answer. Fire away Paddy.'

Paddy: 'Mick, that photo is a picture of which current Manchester United player? I think that it's Beckham, what do you think?'

Mick: 'It's never Beckham. It's obviously Schmeichel.'

Paddy: 'You think so Mick?'

Mick: 'I'm sure.'

Paddy: 'Thanks Mick.'

Chris: 'What a difference of opinion. Do you want to stick on £64,000 or play on for £125,000 Paddy?'

Paddy: 'I want to play on. I am so sure that it's Beckham that I'm going to ignore Mick's advice and go with my first answer. I think it's Beckham.'

Chris: 'Is that your final answer?'

Paddy: 'It is.'

Chris: 'Paddy ... you had £64,000 and you said Beckham. If that is the correct answer you have just won £125,000, however, if it's wrong you go away with £32,000. Paddy (drum roll) Ooh!...it was wrong. Sorry Paddy.

Here is your cheque for £32,000 and you have been a great contestant and a real gambler. Audience please put your hands together for Paddy.'

Paddy: 'Before I go Chris – what was the correct answer, it's killing me?'

Chris: 'Andy Cole.'

Managers Ron Atkinson and Martin O'Neill were being interviewed together on the radio.

Interviewer: 'Ron, what are your main aims this season?'

Ron Atkinson: 'Just to finish mid-table in the Premiership and maintain our position in the top flight.'

Interviewer: 'And what about you Martin?'

Martin: 'We are going to win the league, league cup and FA cup treble. Go on and win the European Cup next year, and turn our finances round so that we make a 50-million profit by having a brand new ground packed to the rafters every game.'

Interviewer: 'That's a bit fanciful isn't it?'

Martin: 'Well Big Ron started it!'

A man went on a game show saying that he could identify which team had used a football, just by smelling it.

The presenter picked up the first ball and held it under the man's nose. 'Newcastle' said the man. 'I can smell their brown ale.' 'Correct' replied the presenter.

The presenter gave the man the next ball, and he had a smell of that one too. 'Derby

County' he exclaimed. 'I can smell the sheep.' 'Correct again!' replied the presenter.

Finally the last ball was passed to the contestant. The man had a good long sniff before saying 'That's an easy one. It's definitely Nottingham Forest.' 'How did you know that one?' asked the amazed presenter. The contestant replied 'I could hear it going down.'

A young Catholic boy from Liverpool went to the Vatican with his mum to see the Pope. He really wanted to meet the Pope, but was worried that he wouldn't stand out amongst the hundreds of other people that were bound to be there. 'Don't worry son' said his mother. 'The Pope is a big football fan, so I'm sure that if you wear your Liverpool shirt the Pope will want to come and talk to you.'

So the following day the boy and his mother were standing in the crowd, and the boy was proudly wearing his Liverpool shirt. As the Pope went past in his Pope-mobile Pope John Paul got out to talk to another little boy who was wearing a Manchester United shirt. He then climbed back into the Pope-mobile and drove straight past the Liverpool fan. The little boy was very upset that he hadn't met the Pope, but his mother reassured him saying 'Don't worry, I'll buy you a Manchester United shirt this afternoon. We'll come back to see the Pope tomorrow and you can wear the Manchester United shirt. The Pope is obviously a big fan of theirs, so he should stop to talk to you.'

They went back to the Vatican the next day, and the boy was very excited at the prospect of meeting the Pope. The Pope-mobile went by, and the boy was delighted to see it stop. He got really excited when the Pope got out and started walking towards him. John Paul bent down to talk to the boy and said 'I thought I told you to f**k off yesterday!'

A very wealthy man wanted to give his sons a present each, so he called them to a meeting and asked them what they wanted. The oldest son asked for a train set, so the father purchased London Underground for him. The second asked for a CD player, so his father bought him a radio station. The final son wanted a cowboy outfit, so his father gave him Everton football club.

A couple went to the ticket office at Plymouth football club and handed over a £20 note and said 'Two please.'

'Thank you' replied the man in the ticket office. 'Would you like the goalkeeper and the centre forward – or are there two different players that you'd prefer?'

Boss: 'And just why are you late for work this morning Simon?'

Simon: 'I'm very sorry Sir. Normally I dream of my favourite football team and wake up at 7am when the game has finished.

Unfortunately this morning my team had to play extra time.'

Striker: 'I had an open goal, but I still didn't manage to get the ball in the net. I could kick myself I'm so upset.'

Manager: 'I wouldn't bother. I expect that you'd miss.'

Birmingham had just signed a brilliant new Romanian football star. On his first match with his new club he scored a hat-trick and was named man of the match. After the match he was ecstatic with his performance, and immediately phoned his mum to tell her his good news.

His mum said 'Well I'm glad to hear that things are going so well for you. Unfortunately though things aren't going so well for us. Our house has been burgled, your father has been beaten up, and your sister was raped and we're feeling pretty low ... I just wish we'd never moved to Birmingham with you.'

The footballer from the country had come on for his first match, but was not performing as well as he was expected to. The physio ran on to the pitch with a message to him from the coach.

'The coach says if you don't improve, he'll pull you off at half time.' 'That's great' replied the country boy, 'we only got oranges at half time at my old club.'

Sleeping with a woman before a match has never harmed any professional footballer's career – it's staying up all night looking for a woman to sleep with that does the damage.

Chris's girlfriend refused to go to football matches with him as she said that it was too political – there was always someone playing on the left wing.

Luton Town's trophy room got burgled last week. Police have issued a statement saying that they are looking for two suspicious characters who were last seen walking quickly away from the ground carrying a rolled up carpet.

Q: What is the difference between Manchester United and Oasis?
A: United are still playing Giggs.

Q: What is the difference between Forest and a teabag?
A: A teabag stays in the cup longer.

Q: What do the premiership and Brazil have in common?
A: Soon there will be no Forest.

Two elderly sisters donated £5 to a charity raffle, and to their surprise they won tickets to a football game. Since they had never been to a football game before they decide that they would like to go.

The day of the match arrived, and the two ladies found themselves in a noisy stadium overlooking a large, grassy expanse. They watched the kick-off and the seemingly endless back and forth struggles that comprised the scoreless first half.

They enjoyed the band music and the entertainment that followed. Then came the second half. When the teams lined up for the kick-off, one of the elderly ladies nudged her sister and said 'We can go home now, after all it was at this point that we came in.'

Last week it was reported that the Scottish football team had been examined by a medical team and pronounced fit for FA.

Q: What is the difference between a triangle and Middlesbrough football club?

A: A triangle has got three points.

SEXY
SPORTSMEN

The footballer performs for 90 minutes with a break at half time. He always expects to score, and shoots from a variety of positions.

The cricketer goes for a good innings but could well be all out for 69 and awaiting reply.

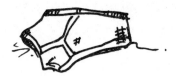

The golfer is a club-swinger who tries to steer clear of the rough, loves to get a few birdies, but a hole in one is even better.

The snooker player pays great attention to every stroke of his cue and rubs the tip before getting down to business with his balls.

The rugby player doesn't score goals with his odd shaped balls, but certainly tries. He will need a bath at the end of play.

The swimmer's breast-stroke is one of his specialities. He puts in several lengths, back and front, before emerging dripping wet.

AT THE
RACES

A group of junior school children accompanied by two female teachers went on a school study trip to the local race course to learn about thoroughbred horses and the supporting industry.

During the tour some of the school children wanted to go to the toilet so it was decided that one teacher would go with the girls, and the other would go with the boys.

Whilst the teacher assigned to the boys was waiting patiently outside the men's loos, one of the boys came outside and explained that he couldn't reach the urinal. The teacher had to go inside and hoist the little boys up by their armpits one at a time.

As she was lifting one boy up, she couldn't help but notice that he was unusually well-endowed for a boy of his age. 'I suppose that you are in the sixth,' she said.

'No I'm not,' he replied. 'I'm in the fifth riding Phantom Prince, but thanks for the lift.'

At the racetrack, a trainer was going through the strategy for the race with his jockey, and seemed to put something in the horse's mouth as a steward passed by.

'What was that?' inquired the steward.

'Nothing,' said the trainer, 'just a lump of sugar. Here have one, and I'll have one too.'

The steward left, and the trainer continued his instructions. 'You can't lose. The only thing that could possibly beat you down the straight is either the steward or me.'

A vicar was desperately trying to raise funds for a new church roof, and decided to buy a racehorse to make some money. However, at the local market all of the race horses were far too expensive, so the vicar decided to buy a donkey instead. He entered it in a race, but wasn't very hopeful as all of the other starters were horses. However, to his immense surprise the donkey finished third.

The next day the headline in the local paper read: 'VICAR'S ASS SHOWS.' The vicar was so pleased with the donkey that he entered it in the races again, and this time it won. The following day's paper read: 'VICAR'S ASS OUT IN FRONT.'

The bishop was outraged by the headlines, and so demanded that the vicar stop entering his donkey in the races. But the headline in the local paper just said: 'BISHOP SCRATCHES VICAR'S ASS.'

Well, this really upset the bishop who ordered the vicar to get rid of his animal. The vicar decided to give the donkey to a nun, who needed funding for her convent. The headlines read: 'NUN HAS BEST ASS IN TOWN.'

The poor bishop was horrified as the headlines just kept getting worse. He made the nun get rid of the donkey too. She sold him to a nearby farmer for £30, and the paper's headline was: 'NUN PEDDLES ASS FOR THIRTY POUNDS.'

Upon reading this, the bishop died of a heart attack. The final headline in the local paper read: 'NUN'S ASS KILLS BISHOP.'

A man was walking his three-legged greyhound in the local park, when he spotted something in the bushes. On closer inspection he realised that it was a lamp, and on giving it a rub a genie appeared. 'I expect you want a wish,' said the genie. 'But I'm bored of giving out wishes all the time, so you can only have one.'

The man had a long think because he was only allowed one wish and he wanted to make it a good one. Finally he said 'Can you make my greyhound a race winner? No one would ever back a three-legged dog, so I'll make a fortune.'

The genie, who was having a bad day said 'I'm a genie, not a miracle-worker, can you think of anything a bit less tricky?'

'OK,' said the bloke. 'I'd really like it if Luton Town won the League as I'm a huge fan of theirs.'

The genie rolled his eyes to the heavens and said 'About that greyhound of yours ...'

A jockey was getting really angry with a horse who always lost races it was expected to win. It was damaging the jockey's career, as everyone was starting to think that the fault lay with him.

'Perhaps it needs an incentive to win,' suggested the horse's owner.

So just before the horse's next race, the jockey warned it that if it lost the race it would never be able to race again, and would have to find another job – probably on a milk round.

The horse neighed at the jockey as if it had understood, and so the jockey felt confident that this time he might actually win something.

However, the horse was soon once again trailing at the back of the pack. The exasperated jockey shouted at the horse and whipped it as well, but the horse just turned its head to the jockey and said 'Take it easy. I've got to be up at the crack of dawn.'

The horse owner was particularly proud of one of his stallions. He was a beautiful horse and was incredibly fast during training. There was just one problem with him – every time he raced he would slow down when he saw a mare so that he could wink at them. The horse owner was furious as the horse was a definite winner as long as they were no mares running. He decided that he would have to have the horse gelded.

The surgery was performed, and a few weeks later the horse was ready to race again. The owner was delighted to see that his eyes weren't wandering at all while he was in the gates. He looked like he was concentrating on the race, with his head poised directly in front of him.

The gun sounded the start of the race and all of the horses charged out except for the owner's horse. He was absolutely livid and immediately ran towards the horse. 'What's the matter with you now?' he screamed at the animal.

'What's the matter with me?' the horse moodily replied. 'How would you feel if you'd just had the operation I had, and then some smart a**e yelled into a loud speaker 'They're off?'

The crafty horse dealer sold one of his horses for a tidy sum after describing it as 'without fault.' But when the unfortunate buyer took it to the vet it transpired that the horse was almost totally blind. The buyer was furious, and angrily demanded of the horse dealer why he had described the animal as 'without fault.'

The horse dealer smoothly replied 'Well of course I said the horse was without fault. It's not his fault if he's blind is it?'

The horse was the cricket team's star batsman. He's been slogging sixes all morning, when the other batsman hit a single and began charging up to the wicket. To the team's dismay however, the horse didn't move from his crease.

'Godammit, run' shouted the irate team captain.

'If I could run' replied the horse, 'I wouldn't be playing cricket, I'd be at the race track.'

'Are you sure that you're a qualified jockey?' enquired the perplexed steward. 'You've just put that saddle on back to front.'

'But how do you know which way I'm going?' replied the snooty jockey.

The girl asked her Dad why horses had six legs when you could only see four.
'Why do you think that a horse has six legs?'
'Well, I read in a book that a horse has forelegs at the front and two legs at the back.'

CRAZY GOLF

'How was your golf game dear?' enquired Tom's wife Annie.

'Well, I was hitting pretty well, but my eyesight's got so bad I couldn't see where the ball went.'

'But you're 75 years old Tom, what do you expect?' asked his wife. 'Why don't you take my brother Fred along with you next time?'

'He's 85 and he's never played golf in his life' replied Tom.

'But he's got perfect eyesight, dear, he could watch your ball for you and tell you where it landed' Annie said.

So the following day Tom teed off with Fred watching out for his golf ball. The ball disappeared straight down the middle of the fairway. 'Did you see where it went to?' Tom enquired. 'Sure did' Fred replied.

'Well where is it then,' said Tom. 'I forgot' was Fred's forlorn reply.

The new golfer came racing into the clubhouse in a total panic. 'I've had a nightmare' he exclaimed. 'I just sliced the ball and it went into the main road, knocking a cyclist of his bike and under the path of a lorry. The lorry ran him over, and then four cars behind the lorry went into the back of each other. There are people lying injured everywhere, and the pile-up might can even worse. What on earth can I do about it?'

The president of the golf club thought hard and then said: 'Well I think that you should take it a bit slower on the backswing.'

Three men had been playing golf together each Sunday for a couple of years. At the end of every game, two of the golfers would go for a shower, whilst the other would go straight to the clubhouse bar for a couple of drinks.

Finally, curiosity got the better of two of the golfers, and they asked the third man why he always dashed straight for the bar every week, rather than first having a shower. 'Well, I'm ashamed to admit it' he replied, 'but I never have a shower at the clubhouse because my penis is so small I would be embarrassed.'

'Does it work?' enquired one of the others.

'Well of course it works' the third golfer said.

'Well, would you like to swap it for one that looks good in the shower?' came the reply.

A man took the day off work and decided to play a game of golf. He was teeing up for the third hole when he noticed a frog sitting next to him. He thought nothing of it, but just as he was taking his swing a voice said 'Ribbit, 9 iron.'

The man looked around, but he couldn't see anyone, so he prepared to take his shot again. 'Ribbit, 9 iron.' The man looked at the frog in amazement, but he wasn't about to have an amphibian prove him wrong. So he put his club away and pulled out a 9 iron instead. He took his shot and hit a birdie. He was totally shocked and said to the frog 'You must be a lucky frog' to which the frog replied 'Ribbit, lucky frog.'

The golfer decided to take the frog with him to the next hole, to see if it would give him any more handy hints. 'What do you think frog?' the golfer enquired as he lined up to take the next shot. 'Ribbit, 3 wood' came the reply. So the man got out a 3 wood and this time he got a hole in one. The man was absolutely ecstatic, and by the end of the day he had played the best game of his life, all thanks to the lucky frog. With the game over he turned to the frog and said 'Where to next?' to which the frog replied 'Ribbit, Las Vegas.'

The frog and the man went to Las Vegas, and the man said to the frog 'What shall we do?' The frog said 'Ribbit, play roulette.' So the man approached the roulette table and said 'What do you think I should bet frog?' The frog answered 'Ribbit, put £3,000 on black six.' It was a million to one that the man would win, put he trusted the frog and decided to do what it had suggested. He won, and loads of money came sliding across the table to him.

The man was so pleased he immediately went and booked the best hotel room in Las Vegas for him and the frog. He sat the frog down and said 'Frog, I don't know how to repay you, you've given me so much good luck, and now I will never have to worry about money again.' So the frog replied 'Ribbit, if you want to repay me, kiss me.' The man thought that that was the least he could do for the helpful frog, so he bent down and kissed it. All of a sudden, the frog then turned into the most beautiful 16-year-old girl.

'And that your honour, is the case for the defence.'

Club officials had been called to the ninth hole, where three men were having a fight. They were alarmed to see that another man lay dead in a bunker nearby. They finally managed to break up the fight, and demanded an explanation for this undignified behaviour.

'Well,' said one of the three, 'that man in the bunker is my partner, David. He just had a stroke, and these two bastards are trying to add it to my score.'

A golfer decided to practise his swing at the driving range after work one evening. He got a large bucket of balls, and hit them one after the other, but no matter how hard he tried, he just kept slicing them. There was no one else practising on the driving range, and he was determined to stay until he was hitting the ball straight. However, he didn't want to pay for a second bucket of balls, so he decided to go out onto the range and pick up some of the balls he'd already hit.

He began filling his pockets with the golf balls that he'd picked up so that he could carry as many as possible back in one go. As he arrived back at the tee, he was dismayed to see a very attractive girl about to start practising too. As he got closer to the tee, he became aware that she was staring open-mouthed at the strange bulges in his trousers. Trying to explain the situation he said to her 'Oh don't worry, they're just golf balls.' Looking very sympathetic the girl replied 'How unfortunate. Is that like tennis elbow?'

The little girl noticed a couple of golf balls in her father's study. 'What are those strange things, Daddy?' she enquired. 'They're golf balls' her father replied.

The following week the girl walked into her father's study to see many more golf balls on his desk. She went up to her Dad and said 'Did you shoot some more golf this weekend Daddy?'

Stevie Wonder and Nick Faldo are in a bar one evening talking about their respective careers. Faldo asked Stevie 'So how is your singing career going then?' To which Stevie replied ' Pretty well, my 'Greatest Hits' album has been a best seller, and I'm about to release some new material. How's the golf going?'

Nick Faldo answered 'It's alright, I've had a few problems recently, but they seem to be over and I'm playing quite well at the moment, with a big tournament coming up.'

Stevie mentioned 'I always find that when I'm not playing so well, if I stop playing for a couple of weeks, I'm usually alright again by the time I resume play.'

Somewhat surprised by this, Faldo enquires 'Do you play golf Stevie?'

'Of course I do, I've been playing every Saturday for years.' Stevie replied.

'But how can you play when you're blind, Stevie?' Faldo asked.

'Well, my caddie stands in the middle of the fairway and calls to me. I listen for the sound of his voice, and then I know where I have to aim. When I reach the ball, the caddie moves nearer the green, and again calls to me, and I just keep aiming towards the direction of his voice.'

Nick Faldo said 'I can see how that might work, Stevie, but how on earth do you putt the ball?'

'That's easy' Stevie replied. 'The caddy just leans right down to the ground by the hole, and again calls out to me. My hearing is very good, so I can accurately pinpoint where his voice is coming from.'

Amazed, Nick enquired 'So what is your handicap?'

'I play off scratch' said Stevie.

Faldo was very impressed and eagerly said 'How about we play a game together some time?'

'Well, I'd like that' Stevie said 'but the thing is

that I only play for money as because I'm blind people never think of me as a serious golf player. In fact I won't play you for less than £100,000 a hole.'

Faldo thought about it for a moment, as £100,000 for every hole was a lot of money, but then he considered that he was a professional player, and that although Stevie played off scratch, he was, after all, blind, so he should be able to beat him. 'Okay' he said 'when do you want to play?'

'Oh, any night suits me' said Stevie.

Managing directors spend their mornings talking about golf in their offices. However, they spend their afternoons talking about work on the golf course.

Delia asked her husband Jeff 'Darling, if I died would you remarry?'

Jeff was very anxious not to offend his wife, and after thinking about this for a while he carefully replied 'After a considerable period of grieving, I might if I met the right person, because everyone needs companionship.'

'But if you got remarried, would she share our house with you?' Delia asked.

Jeff again thought carefully about his answer before saying 'Well, we designed and built some extensions to the house ourselves. We've lived here for many years, and spent a lot of money on the house so that it looks nice. I am very happy here and don't want to move, so I suppose that the answer is yes dear, she would live in this house.'

'But would she sleep in our marital bed with you?' Delia probed further.

'Our bed is new, and is a deluxe model. It cost us £1,500 so I think that she would sleep in it, yes' Jeff replied.

'Well, I suppose that's fair enough' Delia replied, 'but if I died and you got remarried, would your new wife use my golf clubs?'

'Oh no dear' Jeff replied. 'She can't, she's left-handed.'

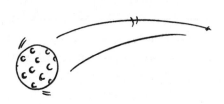

James turned to his caddy when he'd finally finished the 18th hole and said to him 'Tell me honestly, what do you think of my game?'

The caddy smirked as he replied 'Well, your game is quite good, but personally I'll always prefer golf.'

 What goes 'putt, putt, putt?' A very bad golfer.

Two golfers had met for a game of golf over the weekend. They were in a bit of a rush, so agreed that they would only play nine holes instead of the usual 18. One said to the other 'Although we're only playing nine holes instead of 18 we could make it more enjoyable by placing a bet on the outcome, let's put £5 on the lowest score of the round.' The other golfer agreed and they had a highly competitive game which was great fun.

However, after the eighth hole one of the golfers, who was ahead by one stroke sliced his ball into the rough. 'Help me find my ball' he said to the other player. They both searched for about ten minutes to no avail, and the golfer who had hit the ball had realised that a lost ball carried a four-point penalty, meaning that he would lose the bet. He didn't want to lose, so he quickly pulled a new ball out of his pocket, and dropped it onto the ground. 'I've just found my ball' he called out to the other player.

The other player stared at him and slowly shook his head with disgust 'After all the years that we've been friends, I can't believe that you are cheating in a game of golf against me for a measly £5.'

'How dare you say that I've cheated' the golfer replied. 'I found my ball sitting right here in the grass.'

'I can't believe that you're lying to me now as well as having cheated' the other golfer exclaimed. 'I'll have you know that I've been standing on your ball for the last ten minutes.'

Four friends were at the first tee, about to start a round of golf together. The first man said 'This game is costing me dinner with my wife tonight.'

To which the second golfer replied 'That's nothing, I've had to agree to my wife's parents spending the week with us.'

'You think that's bad?' replied the third golfer, 'I had to hand over my credit card to my wife so that she could indulge in some retail therapy.'

The fourth man said 'I don't know what you lot are complaining about. When I woke up this morning, I asked my wife which she would prefer out of a choice of golf course or intercourse. She replied 'Take a sweater' and then went back to sleep.'

The young talented golfer was just about to start a practice round. He had only a few hours spare, so he wanted to get round the course as quickly as he possibly could. He was about to tee off when he was stopped by a very elderly gentleman who asked if he could partner him around the fairway. The golfer didn't want to be rude even though he was in a hurry so he agreed to let the elderly gentleman accompany him.

However, he was amazed to find that the old man played golf quite quickly, despite his advancing years. Eventually, they reached the last hole, and the golfer found himself with a very difficult shot, as a large tree was blocking his path, right between where his ball had landed and the putting green. He took a few minutes to move around the ball, looking for the best angle to take, when the old man piped up 'When I was your age, I could hit the ball right over that tree, on this very hole.'

The young golfer knew that he was a good player, and he wasn't about to be made to look bad by such an elderly player. He swung the ball with great force, and lifted it up to the top of the tree as much as he could, but the ball smacked into the top of the tree trunk and landed right by his feet again. The golfer was furious, both that he had wasted a shot and that he had failed to perform a shot that the old man had managed.

As he looked down at the golf ball in frustration, the old man spoke again 'But obviously, when I was your age that huge tree was only three feet tall.'

The club professional was outraged to see a new golfer gaining an unfair advantage on one of the holes by going to drive off about a metre on the wrong side of the tee. He quickly marched up to the player and said 'Excuse me, but we don't allow cheating of any kind at this golf club.'

'I should hope not' replied the novice golfer, 'but unfortunately this is my second shot.'

A golfer was ready to tee off when a golfer who was on the adjacent fairway hit him right in the head with a golf ball. 'I could have been killed' the golfer shouted out. 'Your ball hit me straight in the head, I'll sue you for five million dollars for that.'

'But I said fore' the other golfer exclaimed.

The first golfer replied 'Okay I'll take it.'

Two friends played golf together regularly but one was considerably better than the other and always won. However, the player who always lost was very proud, and he was determined to win a game.

So one Saturday morning he showed up at the first tee with a huge gorilla and said to his friend 'I have lost every single game I've played against you, but I want to give it one last shot. An acquaintance of mine told me about a golfing gorilla, so I wondered if you would mind playing him instead of me today? I'd like to play for money, as I have lost hundreds to you over the years. Will you play the gorilla for all the money you've taken from me this year in total? Then I might stand a chance of winning it back.'

His friend considered the proposition for a minute and then said 'I don't see why not, I don't think that a gorilla could be very good at golf.'

So the gorilla and the golfer lined up at the first hole, which was a very straight, long hole. The man hit a beautiful shot which took him well over half way to the green. He stepped back, feeling very please with himself and said to his friend 'Right, I'd like to see your gorilla do better than that.' Well, the gorilla took a few practice swings before walloping the ball straight down the middle of the fairway. The golfer looked on in despair as the ball finally landed about one foot from the hole.

The golfer realised that he didn't stand a chance of winning when the gorilla could perform shots like that, so he turned to his friend and said 'I must say, I didn't believe that a gorilla could play golf, but he's exceptional.

There's no point me playing a whole round, when I've already seen what he can do, it would be too humiliating to lose. Let's go to the clubhouse and I'll write you a cheque for the money I owe you.'

The golfer handed over the cheque to his friend, and commiserated his loss with a large whiskey. He then turned to his friend and said 'So how's that gorilla's putting then?' To which his friend replied 'It's exactly the same as his driving.' 'So he is really good then?' enquired the golfer. 'No' his friend answered, 'I meant that his putting is exactly the same as his driving, he hits it hard and long, straight down the middle.'

A father phoned the doctor, very concerned about his child. 'Doctor, my baby just swallowed one of my golf tees.'

'Okay,' the doctor replied. 'I'll be there as soon as I can.'

'Is there anything that I should do whilst we're waiting for you to arrive?' the worried father enquired.

'Just practice your putting' came the reply.

Four friends regularly played golf together at the weekends. One of the four was thought of as a bit of a show off by the others as he would play left handed for a while, and then suddenly he would switch to playing right-handed for a bit – although there appeared to be no logical reason behind the switch. Also, on occasions he would turn up to tee off 20 minutes late.

One morning the four players were at the third hole, and the show off had switched to playing right-handed at the beginning of play. His second shot at the third hole landed just a few inches from the tee, and finally one of his playing partners had to know just why he switched from left to right-handed play so regularly. 'Why do you switch hands all the time? It's driving me mad' he exclaimed. 'Well, every morning when I wake up before playing golf, I look at my wife sleeping in bed. If she is sleeping on her right-hand side, then I play right handed, but if she is sleeping on her left hand side then I play left-handed.'

'I can understand that' the other player replied, 'but what do you do if she's laying on her back?' 'That's when I'm 20 minutes late to tee off' the show-off replied.

A sign at the first tee stated:
'Men: No shirt, no golf. Women: No shirt, no greens fee.'

The two Irish golfers, Paddy and Connor were teeing off at the first, but there was a thick fog over the course making it difficult to see. Paddy hit the ball off into the fog, and then Connor did the same. They then found their way to the putting green to search for their golf balls.

When they find both balls, they discover that one is a long way off the putting green, whilst the other is only a few inches away from the hole. They had both used the same make of golf ball, and as they hadn't been able to see the flight of their golf balls through the fog, they didn't know which ball belonged to them. They spent a long time arguing about it, before the club professional appeared to help them decide.

After congratulating both players on great shots, considering the difficult conditions of play, the club pro simply said 'Well, which one of you was playing with the orange ball?'

Brian was a terrible golfer but he was very wealthy and enjoyed spending money on his hobby. One morning he decided to treat himself, and spent a considerable amount of money hiring a caddy to go round the course with him. However, this luxury didn't make any difference to his ability, and he played poorly all day.

As he approached the 14th hole, to his horror he saw a huge lake, which he knew that he was bound to hit his golf ball into. He turned to the caddy and said 'I've played so badly, I might just as well go and drown myself in that lake.' 'I wouldn't bother if I were you' the caddy replied. 'I don't think you'd be able to keep your head down long enough.'

Last Saturday Chris went out to play a round of golf and ended up hitting two of his best balls. He stood on a rake.

Two serious golf players were teeing off at the seventh. The first had driven his ball a long way down the fairway, but the second hit his ball a little too hard. Just as it flew through the air another golfer wandered out across the grass, and into the path of the oncoming ball. It hit him right in the forehead, and he dropped down dead from the force of the ball. The second golfer was in a terrible state at causing this man's untimely death and yelled out to his golfing partner, 'What on earth am I going to do? There's blood everywhere, and the man is definitely dead.'

The first golfer looked at his friend and replied 'It's not as bad as it looks. I'm sure that a pitching wedge will get that ball free.'

The Scotsman and the American were discussing golf together. 'In the US we don't play in winter because the course is too hard.

We wait until spring to play when the weather is better' the American commented.

'Ye big pansies' the Scotsman replied. 'We don't let the snow and the cold weather bother us in Scotland.'

'But how do you play in the snow?' the American enquired. 'Do you paint your balls black?'

'Don't be ridiculous' replied the surprised Scotsman, 'We just put on a pair of thick thermals.'

Isn't it strange how men blame fate for all of their accidents, but don't mind claiming full responsibility for a hole in one.

A man was out on the golf course when he saw a genie at the fifth tee. The genie agreed to grant him one wish. He thought for a while and then said 'Well, there is one thing, I've always wanted a bigger willy. It would give me so much confidence, and I'm sure that my wife would be really pleased by the change.' The genie granted the golfer his wish and then disappeared.

As the man continued his round of golf, he became aware that a change was occurring in his size. By the next hole it was down to his knee, and by the end of the round it was touching the top of his socks. He quickly ran back to where he had met the genie. 'Is something wrong?' enquired the genie. 'Yes' the golfer answered, 'can I please have one more wish.' 'And what would that be?' the genie laughingly asked. 'Could you make my legs longer please?'

THOUGHTS ON THE GAME OF GOLF:

In primitive society when native tribes beat the ground with clubs and yelled, it was called witchcraft. However today, in civilised society, it is called golf.

Golf is a game in which the slowest people in the world always seem to be in front of you, whereas the fastest people in the world always seem to be behind you.

Golf is an expensive way of playing marbles. The amateur golfer often prefers the golf cart to the caddy. It has been suggested that this is because the cart cannot count, criticise or laugh.

The secret of good golf is to hit the ball hard, straight and not too often.

Golf is a five-mile walk punctuated with disappointments.

An amateur golfer is one who addresses the ball twice. Once before swinging, and once again after swinging.

There is no game like golf. You go out with three friends, play 18 holes and before you know it you've returned with three enemies.

Once upon a time golf was a rich man's sport, but now it has millions of poor players.

20 LAWS OF GOLF:

LAW 1: No matter how bad your last shot was, the worst is yet to come. This law doesn't expire on the 18th hole since it has the supernatural ability to extend over a whole tournament, an entire summer, and eventually throughout a player's lifetime.

LAW 2: Your best round of golf will be followed almost immediately by your worst ever round of golf. The probability of the latter increases dramatically every time you tell somebody about the former.

LAW 3: Brand new golf balls are water magnetic. This has not yet been scientifically proven, but nevertheless it is a known fact that the more expensive a ball is, the greater its attraction to water.

LAW 4: Golf balls will never bounce off trees and back into play. If a miracle should occur and your ball should bounce back into play, expect the tree to be felled by a bolt of lightning about ten seconds later.

LAW 5: No matter what caused a golfer to mess up a particular shot, all of his playing partners must immediately say 'You looked up' whilst sadly shaking their heads.

LAW 6: Sand is alive. Otherwise how can anyone explain the way that it works against the golfer?

LAW 7: A golfer hitting into your group will always be bigger than every member of your group. Conversely, a group that you accidentally hit into will invariably consist of a 17-stone rugby player or a convicted felon.

LAW 8: The person that you would most hate to lose to will always be the person who consistently beats you.

LAW 9: The higher a golfer's handicap is, the more qualified he thinks he is as an instructor.

LAW 10: Golf carts always break down when you have a bad back, and are at the part of the course that is furthest away from the clubhouse.

LAW 11: Trees are well known for eating golf balls. There is no possible explanation for this, it is just one of those things.

LAW 12: Golf balls from the same pack will often follow each other. This is more common if the first ball lands in a bunker, or in the water.

LAW 13: Every par-three hole has, without exception, a desire to totally humiliate players.

The shorter the hole is, the greater this desire becomes.

LAW 14: A severe slice is a thing of wondrous beauty and power.

LAW 15: The last two holes of a round of golf will automatically adjust your score to what it should be.

LAW 16: Topping a three-iron is the most painful torture known to man.

LAW 17: All three-woods are demon-possessed.

LAW 18: 'Nice lag' can usually be translated to mean 'lousy putt.' Similarly, 'tough break' usually means 'Ha! You missed an easy one there, sucker.'

LAW 19: Golf should be given up at least twice every month.

LAW 20: All vows taken on a golf course shall be valid only until the sunset of the same day.

REALLY RIOTOUS RUGBY HUMOUR

A man was walking down the road when he heard a woman screaming and realised that there was a smell of burning in the air. He ran around the street corner to see a huge crowd of people gathered in front of a burning building.

There was a lady trapped in the building who was leaning out of the window with a new-born baby in her arms, begging passers by to save her child.

The man stepped below the window and yelled 'Throw down the baby, I'll catch her.' But the woman replied 'No you'll drop her.' 'No I won't' the man answered. 'I play rugby for the England national team, and I've been picked for every international match in the last seven years. I've never missed a pass, so there's no way I'll drop your baby.'

The woman thought that this sounded like her best chance to save her baby, but she had better check the man's story one more time. 'Are you sure you have never missed a single pass?' she enquired. 'No never' the rugby player assured her. 'Also, I have been voted best international rugby player for three years in a row. So you really can trust me with your baby.'

The woman looked at the walls of the building, which by now had fire going all up them, and decided that she didn't have a choice in the matter, and that she would just have to entrust her baby's life to the rugby player. 'Okay, here she comes' she shouted down, and with that she gently let go of her baby.

The rugby star sprang into action leaping up into the air, as if he was in a lineout, however the wind was carrying the young child off course. The rugby player arched his body into the direction of the child and incredibly managed to catch her safely in his arms. As the crowd was going wild with applause for the man's heroic deed, and the mother was shouting out her thanks to him, the rugby player sadly lost track of what he was doing.

The crowd watched with horror as the rugby player calmly raised one arm before proceeding to drop-kick the baby over the nearby electricity pylons.

A rugby player has recently been jailed for a year for biting an opponent's ear off. At the end of the hearing the judge ruled that this was 'not within the normal give-and-take that the game allowed.'

Tim and Ben were discussing the state of the rugby club's social club. 'I understand that the social club is looking for a treasurer' Tim said.

'Yes, we are' Ben replied.

'But I was sure that the position of treasurer was only filled last month' Tim exclaimed.

'Well yes, that's correct' Ben answered. 'That is the treasurer we are looking for.'

Ted and Robert were bemoaning the fact that they hadn't managed to get a ticket for the rugby cup final. The gates to the ground had been slammed shut just as they had reached the front of the queue.

The ground was so full that no-one wanted to join the huge queue for the toilets, so most of the male fans made their way to the gates, where they could pee through the bars.

As they were complaining about missing the most important game of the season, Ted suddenly noticed that several willies were poking through the gate. 'Look, here's a chance to improve our luck today by making a bit of money' he said to Robert. He grabbed one of the willies and said 'if you don't throw a fiver over the gate, I'll cut your willy off.'

To Ted and Robert's surprise a fiver fluttered down over the fence. 'We're going to make a packet!' Ted exclaimed to Robert. 'We'll go around the ground in opposite directions, stopping at all of the gates until we meet back at the middle.'

Twenty minutes later the two met up on the opposite side of the ground. 'I've got nearly £50' said Ted. 'How did you do?' 'Not quite as well as you' Robert replied. 'I've only got about £40. But I did get three willies as well.'

A definition has been given for the three different types of football:

In soccer you kick the ball, in rugby you kick the man if you cannot kick the ball, and in Gaelic football you kick the ball if you cannot kick the man.

HOWZAT!

Two aliens had just returned from Earth after examining the local way of life and customs. They told the rest of the aliens about a very peculiar religious ceremony that they had witnessed during their time on Earth. 'We went to a large green area that was shaped like a crater. There were thousands of worshippers gathered around the outside of the green area. After all of the worshippers had taken their seats two priests walked out onto the centre of the green area, where there was a rectangular area marked out in white on the ground. At each end of the white rectangle there were three wooden spears hammered into the ground, and the spears were linked by two small tubes which rested on top of them.

Then 11 more priests walked onto the green and they were all wearing white robes. Finally two high priests came out wielding clubs and walked onto the white rectangular area. One of the white-robed priests produced a red orb which he then threw at the high-priests with the clubs.'

'That's amazing' said one of the aliens. 'But what happened next?' The first alien replied 'Well every time they got to that point, it started to rain.'

The amateur cricket player's wife rang the club during a match, and was told that her husband had just gone into bat.

'That's okay' she replied. 'I'll hold.'

The American tourist had been advised to go to a cricket match while he was in England. He watched with pleasure as the teams came onto the pitch and the batsman scored four runs off the first six balls. Then the umpire called 'Over.'

'Well' he remarked as he got up, 'It's a nice game, but it's very short.'

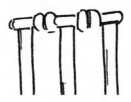

The bowler was up against a stonewaller who never moved his bat. Every ball either hit the bat or passed harmlessly by without the batter attempting a single stroke.

The frustrated bowler turned to the umpire and said 'Is he out if he doesn't move his bat?'

'No' replied the umpire. 'But he certainly will be if he does.'

It was an exciting cricket match, and the championship depended upon the result. George was sitting tensely in front of the television, watching every stroke.

His wife didn't know much about cricket, but she was very patient. 'Why is it so important George?' she enquired. 'I thought they decided who were the champions last year.'

At the break for lunch the spectators and players alike rushed to the bar, where the publican had a special price on pints of light ale. The price per pint was so cheap that everyone decided to drink that rather than their usual.

Unfortunately, the ale was off and halfway through the second innings everyone was so ill that they abandoned the match. It was a case of bad light stopping play.

'It's very simple' said the team captain to the first-time umpire. 'When I shout 'OWZAT!' you simply put up your finger and say 'OUT'. When it's our turn to bat however, I'll tell you a little bit more!'

Just before an important international match was about to start the ground manager got a message from the turnstiles. 'There is a man here who says he wants to come in for free. He's with two friends and he claims that he's an umpire.'

'Don't let them in' the manager instructed. 'The man is obviously lying. Who ever heard of an umpire with two friends?'

The man asked his cricket playing friend 'How do you manage to keep so fit for the season?'

'I think nothing of getting up at five, running around the park for two hours, then getting in three or four hours net practice before a cold bath' the friend replied.

'What a coincidence' his friend said. 'I don't think much of it either.'

The famous English international was being interviewed on television. 'I would agree that I didn't score as much as I should have done in the West Indies' to which the West Indian barmaid who was watching television remarked 'that's not what I heard.'

The dedicated batsman was up against the fast bowler and he was doing exceptionally well. He had just notched up a century when a note was brought out to him, and the game was interrupted whilst he read it. After reading it he called over the umpire and said 'I've just been informed that my wife has been taken to hospital. Do you think you could ask the bowler to shorten his run-up?'

Laura was only a cricketer's daughter, but she could take a full toss in the crease.

'I'm proud to say that in 30 years of playing cricket, I've never scored less than 25 runs, and never taken less than three wickets' Paul exclaimed.

'I wish that I could say the same' Stuart said.

'Well, why don't you?' enquired Jonny. 'Paul just did.'

An expectant father rang the hospital to see how his wife was doing. Unfortunately, the operator mistakenly put him through to Lord's cricket ground. 'How are things going?' the father-to-be enquired.

'Very well' came the reply. 'We've got three out, and hope to have the rest out by lunchtime. The last one was a duck.'

A cricket fan died and ended up in Hell. He'd been there a week when the Devil approached him and said 'What do you feel like doing today? You can do whatever you like.'

'Okay' the man replied. 'I'd love to play cricket, can we play a game?'

'Of course we can' said the Devil, and they went off to get changed. They arrived a bit later at a beautiful pitch and the batsman took up his position but nothing happened.

'Well you see' said the Devil 'that's the Hell of it. We haven't got any balls.'

In his English lesson little Dominic was asked to spell the word 'bowling.' He handed in his answer 'boelin' to the teacher.

His teacher called him out to the front of the class and said 'that is the worst spell of bowling I've ever seen.'

The two cricket club members were discussing their respective marriages.

'So you had a hard game explaining Saturday's cricket match to your wife did you?'

'I certainly did' his friend replied. 'She found out that I wasn't there.'

The avid cricket fan had forced his wife and child to come with him to watch a match. He watched with interest, but they were obviously bored, and couldn't stop fidgeting in their seats.

After a while however the child brightened and turned to her mother. 'They just shouted out "over" she said. 'I know dear' her mother replied. 'But don't take any notice. It keeps going on and on.'

GONE FISHING

A nun had just caught a huge, unusual looking fish. A fisherman saw it and remarked 'Wow, what a nice Gauddam fish.'

'You must not take the Lord's name in vain' said the nun.

'I wasn't replied the fisherman. 'The species of fish you have caught is called the Gauddam fish.'

So the nun took the fish back to the convent and said 'Mother Superior, look at this Gauddam fish I have caught.'

The shocked Mother Superior replied 'Sister you should know better than to use that kind of language.'

'You don't understand' replied the nun. 'That is the name of this particular species of fish. It is known as a Gauddam fish.'

'Give it to me and I shall clean it' said the Mother Superior. Whilst she was cleaning the fish the Monsignor walked in. 'Monsignor' said the Mother Superior, 'look at the Gauddam fish that the sister caught.'

'Mother Superior!' said the Monsignor rather taken aback. 'You must not say such things.'

'But it is the species of fish Monsignor' replied the Mother Superior. 'It's a Gauddam fish.'

'In that case' said the Monsignor 'give me the Gauddam fish and I'll cook it.'

At dinner that night, there was a new priest at

the table, and he remarked on the lovely looking fish.

'Thank you' said the nun. 'I caught the Gauddam fish.'

'And I cleaned the Gauddam fish' said the Mother Superior.

'And I cooked the Gauddam fish' said the Monsignor.

The priest looked around the table in total disbelief, and finally said 'Well then let's eat the fu**ing thing.'

Colin was fishing when he hauled up a little pot. He gave it a rub and as luck would have it, a genie popped out.

'I've been in that pot for five thousand years' said the genie, 'so I'm very grateful to you for letting me out. Therefore, I have decided to give you three wishes.'

Colin dashed home to tell his wife Susan of their good fortune, and they decided that they would go to the shops to see if there was anything nice there for them to wish for.

However, Susan was hungry so she decided that they should get something to eat first. Susan got a tin of beans down from the cupboard but she couldn't remember where she had put the tin opener.

'I wish I could find that tin opener' she exclaimed. With that Whoosh! – it landed in her hand.

'You idiot' exclaimed Colin. 'You wasted one of our wishes on a bloody tin opener. I wish it was up your arse.'

It took their last wish to get it back out again.

Roger was a passionate fisherman, and he would often spend his weekends at the river regardless of the weather. One weekend he headed off as usual but the weather was particularly bad with heavy rain and hailstorms, so uncharacteristically he headed back for home. He was surprised to find his wife still in bed when he returned, so he decided to make a cup of tea for them both. He took it into the bedroom and said to his wife 'Hi darling. I've made us some tea. It's horrible weather out there.'

'Yes I know' replied his wife. 'and that stupid husband of mine has gone out fishing in it.'

The two fishermen, Pat and Dennis had been out fishing when their boat began to sink. Pat realised that Dennis couldn't swim and so he instructed Dennis to climb on his back and he'd swim both of them to shore. However, after an hour Pat was absolutely exhausted. 'Try to swim a few strokes by yourself' he told Dennis. 'If I let go of you I'll drown' replied a frightened Dennis.

They struggled on, and Pat was pleased to see that Dennis was moving his arms to help them through the water. Eventually they reached the shore, and staggered up the beach where Pat collapsed in a heap. 'I'm fu**ed' he moaned.

'I'm sorry' replied Dennis. 'It was the only way that I could hold on.'

Two friends were out fishing for the day when a ravishing young woman ran past them stark naked and laughing maniacally. One of the fishermen was put off his cast, but managed to continue nonetheless.

As he was about to cast again two men in white coats dashed past, they were obviously racing each other and were also laughing. They were less of a distraction, and the fisherman was just about to continue when a third bloke ran past, panting and carrying a bucket full of sand in each hand.

The fisherman had by now totally lost what little concentration he had left, so he turned to his friend and asked 'Do you have any idea what could possibly be going on?'

'Yes' replied his friend. 'There is a mental asylum near here. Every Thursday around this time the woman escapes, rips off all of her clothes and runs to the river. The three men running after her are the nurses. They have a race to see who can catch the woman first, as she will usually insist on having wild sex with her captor before agreeing to go back.'

'Fair enough,' said the fisherman, 'but that doesn't explain why one of the nurses was carrying two heavy buckets of sand.'

'Well,' replied the friend 'that's the lucky nurse who caught her last week. The buckets of sand are his handicap.'

The keen fisherman settled down at his regular spot and waited for the fish to bite. He'd been there for almost two hours without a single catch when a young boy sat down next to him and cast his rod into the water. It only took about one minute before the little boy pulled a huge pike fish from the water.

The fisherman was astounded, but put it down to beginner's luck. However, a few minutes later the boy was pulling another large fish out of the river. This went on and on until finally the increasingly despondent fisherman had to say something.

He leant over to the boy and said 'I've been here for two hours without catching a single thing. You've only been here for about five minutes and already you caught about a dozen fish. How are you doing it?'

The boy replied 'Roo raf roo reep ra rorms rrarm.'

'I can't understand a word you're saying' said the confused fisherman.

The boy spat into his hand and said 'I said you have to keep the worms warm.'

A man and his wife had decided to take up golf, and booked themselves some joint lessons. They met the club professional and headed off to the first tee. The pro told the man to take a swing and see how far he could hit the ball. He hit it about 100 yards and the golf pro said 'Well, that's not a bad first shot, but now try holding the club as firmly as you hold your wife's breasts whilst you take your shot.'

The man did what his instructor had suggested, and hit the ball about 300 yards. The golf pro said 'That's excellent. Remember to always hold the club as tightly as you hold your wife's breasts, and you'll have no problems.'

Next it was the turn of the man's wife. She took her best shot and the ball went 35 yards. The golf pro responded 'That was quite a good shot, but I think that you'd do much better if you held the club like you hold your husband's dick.'

The woman had seen how much her husband had improved his shot when he followed the pro's instruction, so she did as he had said. However, to her surprise the ball only went 10 yards. The golf pro's reply was 'Okay, that wasn't too bad, but now try taking the golf club out of your mouth when you hit the ball.'

Helen and Jacquie met each other at the golf club. 'I hear that you and Steven were recently overseas' Helen remarked.

'That's right' Jacquie replied, 'we have just got back. Steven insisted that we go to the Holy Land. I had the worst time of my life.'

Helen asked 'Why did you have the worst time of your life? I've been to the Middle East myself and I had a fantastic time there.'

'Who said anything about the Middle East?' Jacquie said. 'This was one of Steven's trips. We didn't go to the Middle East, we went to St. Andrew's.'

The club professional was a great teacher, but some of the club members felt that he over-corrected faults. The best example of this came when a young lady approached him to help her correct the fact that she always sliced the ball. He worked on her every day for a month, and now she's the biggest hooker in the district.

Emma said that her golf game was improving. After all she had just hit the ball in one.

Three men were about to tee off together when they were asked if they would mind if a fourth person joined them. They all turned around to see a beautiful blonde woman with amazingly long legs standing there, and immediately all agreed to play with her. They started to tee off one at a time, and as they were doing so the blonde said 'I'm not very good at golf, so I'd appreciate it if you would be patient.' 'Of course we will' the men replied.

However, the blonde then managed to hit a nice shot down the middle of the fairway, and with her second shot she made it on to the green. She turned to the men and said 'I have never got a birdie in my life. If one of you will help me to get a birdie at this hole I will perform oral sex on whoever is the most helpful.'

The first gentleman immediately raced up to her and said 'Aim your putt five inches to the left, and then it will definitely go in the hole.'

The second gentleman then said 'No that's wrong. You must aim about three and a half inches to the right, and then it will definitely go in and you will get a birdie.'

The third gentleman just said 'Just pick the ball up, honey. It's a gimme.'

Two golfers were having a very slow round of golf due to the two ladies in front of them. The two ladies were ambling along, and hit their balls into every bunker and rough patch possible. They also did not wave the two men through, which was proper golf etiquette.

By the ninth hole, the men were fed up of waiting for these two women, and so one of the men said 'I think I'll just go up there and ask those two ladies if they'd mind letting us through, so we can finish our game at our own pace.' However, he only got half way towards them before he started running back. 'I can't ask them' he explained. 'One is my wife, and the other lady is my mistress. Would you mind asking them instead?'

So the other golfer walked towards the ladies, but he too stopped and half way and started to walk back towards his playing partner. He smiled sheepishly at him, before explaining 'Small world.'

A husband and wife were playing in a tournament together at their local club. The first hole was a par four and the husband played it first. He hit a beautiful tee shot right down the middle of the fairway. When they got to the ball his wife took out her golf club and hit the ball three yards into a nearby bunker. Her husband then took his club and hit a lovely shot out of the bunker which landed on the edge of the green. His wife then took out her putter and blasted the ball through the green where it landed in a bunker just past the green. Her husband bit his lip and managed to say nothing. He took out his sand wedge and played a wonderful shot out of the bunker which landed right in the hole.

After finishing the hole the husband could stay quiet no longer. 'I can't believe that we have started this tournament with a bogey' he moaned.

'Don't get angry with me' his wife replied. 'Only two of those shots were mine.'

The club professional was trying to teach a young lady the correct golfing stance. He moved behind her and reached round to show her the right grip. But unfortunately the movement of a few practice swings in this position meant that the zipper of his trouser fly got stuck to the zip on the back of her skirt. They were stuck together in a very embarrassing position, but try as they might they couldn't free themselves.

They were in the middle of waddling over to the club house to get help when a large sheep dog threw a bucket of cold water over them.

Sally came home from the golf course looking pleased with herself.

'How was your lesson?' her husband enquired.

'Great thanks' Sally replied. 'I'm not missing the ball by nearly as much anymore.'

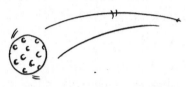

The sensitive woman golfer couldn't help but extend her sympathy to the unhappy looking Scotsman at the end of the clubhouse bar. She was especially moved by the black armband around his shirt sleeve.

'Let me console you' she said, putting an arm over his shoulder.

'Och lassie,' he said brightening up, 'don't be telling me you've found my ball?'

The oldest member of the club arrived in the clubhouse to look for a playing partner. The only person in the clubhouse though was a leggy blonde. However, much to his surprise, she agreed to partner him.

He hit a lovely shot off the first tee, and the blonde said 'That's a terrific shot considering your handicap.'

'My age isn't my only handicap, you know'

the old man replied. 'I've got a wooden arm too.' 'I don't believe you' said the blonde. 'Prove it.' So the old man rolled up his sleeve and unscrewed his wooden arm.

At the next hole, the old man again hit a fantastic drive, and the blonde said 'that was a good shot considering your handicaps.'
'There's more to it than that' the old man replied. 'I've got a wooden leg as well.' 'Prove it' the blonde said, so the old man rolled up his trouser leg and unscrewed his wooden leg.
Again he hit a good shot, and the blonde said 'You're an amazing player considering your handicaps.'
'I have another handicap' said the old man. 'I have a wooden heart.' 'That is impossible' said the blonde. 'Nobody has a wooden heart.' The old man was about to unbutton his shirt when he said 'come behind this bush with me, and then I'll show you my wooden heart.'

20 minutes later a group of friends were playing the hole where the old man and blonde were hidden, when they peered behind the bush and saw their oldest member screwing his heart out.

The two women golfers were playing a round of golf one morning. The first woman teed up to her ball, swung her club and watched as her ball took off at a 90-degree angle. It flew about 20 yards before hitting a rock, bouncing off a tree and then finally coming to rest in the middle of the fairway.

Her friend stared at her and said 'Why didn't you tell me that you had been practising?'

A wealthy couple had recently moved to a new area, and decided to apply for membership to the local private golf club. The golf club was very exclusive, and after a tour of the course, the couple had an appointment with the membership committee. The couple were very nervous as they had to give a good impression to the membership committee if they were going to be asked to join the club. Things were going quite well until one of the committee members asked the wife a question.

'The committee would be interested to hear what you think of the legendary George Warren' the committee member said.

'Well, I think he's great' the wife hurriedly replied. She had absolutely no idea who George Warren was, but she had to try to impress the board. 'I was especially impressed by the way he got out of that bunker on the 12th last week in the tournament.'

As she spoke she saw her husband slump in his chair, and realised that she had made a big mistake. As they drove home after the meeting she turned to her husband and said 'I'm sorry darling, I didn't know what else to say.'

'You've ruined our chances of being accepted now' he muttered. 'Everyone knows that there is no bunker on the 12th hole.'

Three women were playing a quick round of golf one afternoon. As they approached the green on the 14th hole they heard a rustling noise coming from the bushes at the side of the green. One of the women went to see what was making the noise.

'What was it?' the other women enquired.

'Well, you won't believe this' she replied, 'but there is a man standing in the bushes peeing.'

'That's horrible' the others cried. 'Could you see who it was?'

'I couldn't tell as the bushes blocked his face, but I can definitely say that it isn't my husband' the first woman replied.

'Well, I'll go and have a look and see if I recognise him' one of the other women said. She returned a few minutes later and said 'You were right about the bushes being in the way, but I'm fairly sure that it isn't my husband either.'

'Well, I'll go and see if I can recognise the man then' the third woman said, and she too went over to the bush.

'Were you able to tell who it was?' the others asked her when she returned.

'No,' she replied, 'but I can say that not only is it definitely not my husband, but he is also definitely not a member of this golf club.'

A husband and wife were on the tenth fairway and were about to hit their approach shots to the green. All of a sudden a golf ball whizzed past them, missing the husband by a matter of inches. A few minutes later a woman dashed up to them to retrieve her golf ball.

'Are you mad?' the wife screamed at the woman. 'You just hit a terrible shot and you didn't even think to yell 'Fore'. You nearly hit my husband.'

'I'm ever so sorry' the woman replied. She then gave the wife her club. 'Here' she said, 'take a shot at mine.'

A group of women golfers teed off on the 11th hole at their local course. Their tee shots were all wayward, so they ended up in the rough waiting for the group in front of them to finish the hole.

Suddenly a ball landed right in the middle of them, nearly hitting one of them on the back of the head. They turned around to see two men standing on the tee behind them. They finished playing the hole and then waited on the green for the men to arrive.

'Excuse me' one of the women called out as the men approached them, 'but you should look to see if anyone is playing in front of you before you tee off.'

'I'm very sorry' one of the men replied, 'but I didn't have time to yell 'Fore' before I hit the ball.'

'Well you seemed to have time to yell 'Damn' afterwards' a second woman replied.

QUICK QUOTATIONS

'I spent a lot of money on booze, birds and fast cars. The rest I just squandered.'
George Best.

'Ardilles strokes the ball like it is part of his own anatomy.'
Jimmy Magee, RTE.

'My biggest mistake was not taking Eileen Drewery to the World Cup finals.'
Glenn Hoddle.

'I'm not sure Michael Owen is a natural-born goal-scorer.'
Glenn Hoddle.

'Okay, so we lost, but good things can come from it – negative and positive.'
Glenn Hoddle on England's defeat by Chile.

'There'll be no siestas in Madrid tonight.'
Kevin Keegan.

'I thought I was doing quite a good job there.'
Roy Hodgson on his sacking from Blackburn.

'A great performance from Darren Anderton. There are those who've had his critics, but not tonight.'
Brian Moore.

'The World Cup is every four years, so it's going to be a perennial problem.'
Gary Lineker.

'England bowed out of the World Cup last night with their heads held high.'
Bruce Millington, *Racing Post*.

'I'd like to play for an Italian club, like Barcelona.'
Mark Draper (Aston Villa).

'Fortunately, Paul Scholes' injury wasn't as bad as we'd hoped for.'
Trevor Brooking.

'If history repeats itself, I should think we can expect the same thing again.'
Terry Venables.

'To play Holland, you have to play the Dutch.'
Ruud Gullit.

'It took a lot of bottle for Tony (Adams) to own up.'
Ian Wright, commenting on his team mate's alcoholism.

'He dribbles a lot and the opposition don't like it – you can see it all over their faces.'
Ron Atkinson.

'Well, either side could win it, or it could be a draw.'
Ron Atkinson.

'I couldn't settle in Italy – it was like living in a foreign country.'
Ian Rush.

'Gary always weighed up his options, especially when he had no choice.'
Kevin Keegan, Radio 5 Live.

'We'll still be happy if we lose. It's on at the same time as the Beer Festival.'
Noel O'Mahoney, Cork City boss before the game in Munich.

'You must be as strong in March, when the fish are down.'
Gianluca Vialli.

'The gelling period has just started to knit.'
Ray Wilkins.

'The match will be shown on *Match of the Day* this evening. If you don't want to know the result, look away now as we show you Tony Adams lifting the trophy for Arsenal.'
Steve Rider.

'Martin O'Neill, standing, hands on hips, stroking his chin.'
Mike Ingham, Radio 5.

'Big? It's magnificent!'
Alex Ferguson discussing Dion Dublin's member.

'I always used to put my right boot on first, and then obviously my right sock.'
Barry Venison.

'Literally he hasn't got a right foot .... although not literally.'
David Pleat.

'Manchester United have hit the ground running – albeit with a 3-0 defeat.'
Bob Wilson.

'And Seaman, just like a falling oak, manages to change direction.'
John Motson.

'She gives the players a shoulder to talk to.'
Neil Webb talking about Eileen Drewery.

'You can't do better than go away from home and get a draw.'
Kevin Keegan.

'Lombardo speaks much better English than what people realise.'
Mark Goldberg.

'I know the players I want. It is like I have them in the fridge waiting to come out.'
Ruud Gullit.

'What was the last book you read?'
'My own autobiography, which interestingly enough was written by *The Guardian's* Ian Ross.'
Howard Kendall talks to *The Guardian*.

After playing Cameroon in the 1990 World Cup finals: 'We didn't underestimate them. They were just a lot better than we thought.'
Bobby Robson.

'We actually got the winner three minutes from the end but then they equalised.'
Ian McNail.

'We had good ball circulation but not enough penetration.'
Arsene Wenger.

'And for all those of you who watched the last programme (Fanny and Johnny Craddock), I hope that all of your doughnuts turn out like Fanny's.
David Coleman at the start of *Match of the Day*.

'There's only one team that's going to win it now and that's England. I hope I'm not tempting providence there.'
Kevin Keegan, two minutes before Romania's winning goal in the World Cup.

THE
SECOND
INNINGS

The American knew nothing about the game of cricket, but he pretended he did to his English friends. He looked at the end-of-season's averages for his friends' rival team, and every so often he would come across an asterisk and the words 'Signifies not out.'

Finally he turned to his friends and said 'Why don't you get this guy Signifies onto your team? He's never out.'

The cricketer was visiting the psychiatrist. 'It's terrible, doctor, I can't score runs, I'm a terrible bowler, and I can't hold a catch. What should I do?'

'I think you should trying looking for a new career' the psychiatrist replied.

'But I can't' the cricketer answered. 'I'm down to play for England tomorrow.'

In a local match, the umpire was being jeered and heckled unmercifully from the crowd. After a while, he slowly walked over to the boundary and sat down next to his main critic.

'What on earth do you think that you are doing?' the spectator enquired.

'Well,' the umpire replied 'it seems that you get the best view from here.'

The businessman was talking to his friend on the train home after a hard day. 'What a day I've had' he remarked to his friend. 'The office junior asked for the afternoon off to go to his grandmother's funeral. There was an important match on at the cricket ground this afternoon, so I thought that I was on to him, and decided to go along too.'

'That's a good idea' his friend said. 'How was the match?'

'That's where I lost out' the businessman replied. 'It was his grandmother's funeral!'

George and Sally had been married for many years, and as had become usual for a Sunday afternoon, Sally was ironing, whilst George was reading some bowling averages.

'Do you remember the day you proposed to me at that cricket match?' Sally asked. 'You were ever so bold.'

'No I wasn't' George replied. 'I was caught and bowled.'

One Sunday, the Devil challenged God to a cricket match.

'Don't be ridiculous' God said. 'We've got all the cricketers up here.'

'Yes I know' the devil answered. 'But we've got all the umpires.'

The nervous young batsman was having a terrible innings, and was lucky to still be in at the crease. After a while he stammered to the wicket-keeper 'Well I expect you've seen worse players' he said hopefully. However, there was total silence from the wicket keeper.

'I said' the batsman repeated 'I expect

you've seen worse players.'

'I heard you the first time' the wicket-keeper replied. 'I was just trying to think.'

The local club's batsman was rather big-headed, and wildly over-rated his batting ability. He was at the club bar when he was approached by a club member who couldn't resist saying 'You know, whenever I watch you bat I always wonder.'

'I know' the big-head replied 'You wonder how I do it.'

'No' replied the club member. 'Not how you do it, why you do it.'

The two Yorkshiremen were watching the match. One discovered that he'd left his wallet at home and his friend offered to go back and get it for him. He returned 15 minutes later pale and shaken.

'I've got terrible news for you Sam. Your wife has run off and left you, and your house has burned to the ground.'

'I've got worse news than that for you' Sam replied. 'Boycott's out.'

The two rival cricketers were boasting. One said to the other 'The local team want me to play for them very badly.'

'Oh well' the other said 'in that case you're just the man for the job.'

The visiting team were surprised to find that there were no scoring facilities at the village ground. The captain approached the village's team captain and asked 'How do you keep score here?'

'We keep it in our heads' replied the villager's captain, who was a big, burly blacksmith. 'If there are any arguments about it, we settle it behind the pavilion after the game.'

It had been a tense game and then the batsman was run out, a decision with which he obviously disagreed. He marched up and down outside the pavilion until the umpire went in to meet him.

'I was not out' the angry batsman exclaimed to the umpire.

'Oh, no?' questioned the umpire. 'Well if you don't believe me then look in the papers tomorrow.'

It was the after lunch session, but the batsman had obviously had a bit too much to drink during the interval. He staggered up to his captain, and admitted that he could see three of everything.

'Don't worry' his captain instructed. 'When the three balls come flying towards you, just make sure that you hit the middle one.'

The batsman wobbled backed to his crease, and did as he had been instructed, but he was bowled first ball.

'What on earth happened, didn't you hit the middle ball?' his angry captain enquired.

'Of course I did' the inebriated batsman replied. 'Unfortunately though I used my outside bat.'

The slip fieldsman had had a very depressing day, during which he had dropped ten catches, all off the same bowler. After the game he was talking to the bowler when he looked at his watch.

'I must dash' he said. 'I have a train to catch.'

'Let's hope you have better luck with that' was the bowler's sour reply.

How does the umpire check the weight of a bail?

He takes it to the bail-weigh station.

A friend asked Jack 'Tell me, is your daughter's fiancèe a good catch?'

'Of course he is' Jack answered. 'He's the best fielder we've got in the side.

The club captain was after some new talent for his team. 'What are you like at wicket-keeping?' he asked one applicant. 'Passable' was the boy's reply.

'We've already got one like that' the captain said. 'I'm looking for one that's impassable.'

During the match, the fieldsman positioned just behind the umpire kept trying to distract the batsman as the ball was bowled to him.

Several appeals for l.b.w. were rejected, and finally the umpire turned to the fieldsman and said sternly 'I've been watching you for the last 20 minutes you know.'

'I thought so' the cheeky fielder replied. 'I could tell that you weren't watching the game.'

The batsman walked up to the crease and carefully took his guard. He looked round the field, noting the position of each player. Then, he slowly patted down several non-existent bumps on the pitch, before finally signalling that he was ready to accept the first delivery.

The ball came thundering down and immediately uprooted the middle stump. 'What a shame' said the wicket-keeper. 'Just as you were getting set.'

The village club had a big-headed captain. He was a below-average player, but considered himself to be the best in the side. They were up against tough opposition, and as they walked out he announced 'I'll open bowling from the pavilion end.'

'Okay, captain' said the fast bowler. 'You bowl them in, and then I'll come on and bowl them out.'

HUMOROUS HUNTERS

In the hunting club two new members were being shown around and introduced to existing members. One old man, snoozing peacefully in a chair was pointed out to them as having been a superb hunter, with some amazing stories to tell of his experiences. The new members were very keen to hear these stories so they woke up the old man and asked him to tell them one of his stories.

'Well,' began the old man, 'I remember back in 1935 a group of friends and I went on a lion-hunting expedition in Africa. We were walking through thick bushes for four days without stopping, and we hadn't seen a single lion. On the fifth day I was exhausted so I rested by a tree and because I was so tired I ended up falling asleep. I was in a deep sleep when I was suddenly awakened by a tremendous noise in the bushes. As I reached for my gun, the biggest lion I had ever seen jumped out of the bushes towards me and went 'ROOAAAARRRRRRR!' and I just s**t myself.'

The new hunting club members were amazed by this exciting story, and one of them said 'I'm not surprised, I would have s**t myself too if a huge lion jumped out at me.'

The old man looked agitated and shook his head. 'No, not then. It was just now when I said ROOAAAARRRRRRR!'

Two hunters were out on a safari expedition in Kenya when they came across some very large lion tracks in the ground. Confronted with the prospect of coming face to face with a lion for the first time, the first hunter turned to the second and said, 'You follow these forward, and trace where the lion has got to. I'll retrace them, so we can ascertain where it has been.'

Keith was new to hunting and had been really looking forward to his first hunting trip. As he walked into a clearing he was astonished to see a young, beautiful woman lying on the ground in the nude.

'Excuse me miss,' said Keith 'are you game?'

The young woman took one look at the rather handsome Keith and replied 'Yes.'

So Keith shot her.

The hunter had spent weeks tracking an enormous bear and finally had him in his sights. He carefully aimed and then fired a shot, and ran through the bush to claim the dead animal. To his dismay there was no bear, and to his horror he was tapped on the shoulder by a very live one.

I am fed up of being shot at all the time by you hunters' said the bear. 'I'm going to teach you all a lesson. You must get down on the floor and give me a blow job. That should put you off shooting bears.'

The terrified hunter did as he was told, but the next day he returned to the bush with a bigger gun determined to kill the animal that had humiliated him so much. On seeing the bear he fired several times and dashed forward to find him dead.

However once more he was tapped on the shoulder by the bear, who simply said 'You know the ritual, down you go.'

The infuriated hunter could take no more, he raced into the bush the following morning with the most powerful and accurate gun that money could buy. This time he was careful to get as close as possible to the bear before firing.

Unbelievably, the bear was once more waiting for him. 'Tell the truth' said the bear, 'you're not in this for the hunting are you?'

Every morning before setting off into the jungle the two hunters put on their big walking boots to get through the rough terrain. However on the morning they were going to look for gorillas one of the hunters put on a pair of trainers instead.

'What are they for?' enquired his hunting partner.

'I don't want to be caught and eaten by a huge gorilla' he replied.

His hunting partner laughed and said 'But you'll never outrun a gorilla in them.'

'I won't have to.' Replied the trainer wearer. 'I'll only have to outrun you.'

Shaun was always boasting about what a great shot he was. His friend Josh was getting bored of his continual boasts, and he decided to bet Shaun that if they went into the woods he would find an animal that Shaun couldn't hit. Shaun was so confident of his abilities that he happily accepted the bet and the next morning the two went off together into the woods.

Josh stopped a squirrel high up at the top of a tree, and as the tree was also quite a distance away he thought that Shaun would never be able to hit it. Taking aim, Shaun fired and a second later they watched as the squirrel raced down the tree.

Josh laughed and said 'Well, it looks like I just won that bet.' 'I don't think so' Shaun replied. 'What you just saw was a miracle.' 'What do you mean by a miracle?' Josh asked.

'Well' Shaun replied 'That squirrel just ran down that tree with its heart shot out.'

Two retired hunters had met at one of their houses for a few whiskeys, and the first remarked to the second 'That's a very impressive stuffed bear you have in your hallway.'

'Why thank you' replied the second hunter. 'I shot that when I went hunting with Morris Hughenden-Smith.'

'What did you stuff the bear with?' enquired the first hunter.

'Morris Hughenden-Smith' replied the second.

Two Irish blokes were hunting ducks. However, despite a whole day hunting they hadn't got a single duck. Finally, as daylight went one turned to the other and said 'Maybe we'd have more success if we threw that dog a little bit higher.'

The hunter was still shaking with fear as he told his friend back at the camp what had just happened to him. 'I found myself running through the outback with a huge grizzly bear chasing after me. He was catching me up with every step, and I could here him snorting behind me. It was obvious that I was to be his dinner. I realised that my gun was out of ammunition and the only refuge in sight was a tree on which the lowest branch was some 20 feet off the ground.'

'Surely you didn't manage to grab that lowest branch?' his friend enquired.

'Yes, on my way down.' The shaking hunter replied.

'Caught you at last' smirked the gamekeeper as he grabbed the poacher. 'I saw you throw that plucked duck into the river as soon as you saw me. It's still floating on the surface, and how do you explain that all its feathers are covering your clothes?'

'Well' replied the poacher, 'the duck wanted to go out for a swim so I'm just looking after it's clothes.'

Paddy and Mick were out hunting ducks, but they had seen a single duck all day. They had been waiting for five hours and were beginning to think that they would never see a duck when suddenly a huge duck flew overhead. Paddy hurriedly picked up his shotgun and aimed it at the bird. With one shot he hit it, and it plummeted straight down to the ground.

'Wasn't that a great shot?' he asked Mick.

'I don't know about that' Mick replied. 'It seems to me that you just wasted a bullet.'

'What makes you say that?' Paddy enquired.

'Well, that duck would have died from the fall alone.'

A man had decided that he wanted to learn how to hunt. After reading about the subject, he realised that he would need a good hunting dog.

He looked through several specialist magazines before he answered one advertisement for hounds which had been placed by a local farmer. The farmer showed him a number of dogs, but the man didn't like any of them. Just as he was about to leave he saw a lovely looking dog that the farmer hadn't shown him. 'Can I see that one?' he asked the farmer. 'I'm afraid not' the farmer replied. 'He is my special hunting dog.' The man asked why the dog was so special, and the farmer said that he would show him.

The man followed as the farmer walked with the dog to a nearby field. He then bent down, lifted up one of the dog's ears and whispered 'Go and find the birds!' The dog immediately raced to some nearby bushes and barked once whilst he was standing in front of them. 'That means that there is one bird in that bush' the farmer explained. The man didn't believe him, so the farmer hit the bush and a huge pheasant flew out.

The farmer thought that the man needed more convincing of his dog's talent, so he bent down and whispered into the dog's ear 'Go and find the birds!' The dog ran at top speed to another bush. He stopped directly in front of it and barked twice. 'That means that there are two birds in that bush' the farmer told the man. With that, he hit the bush and two huge pheasants flew away.

The man thought how successful he would be at his new pastime if he bought the dog, so he asked the farmer if he could buy him. The farmer said that it would cost the man a lot of money, as he didn't really want to part with his pet, but in the end they reached an agreeable sum. The man went home with the dog.

About a month later the farmer was going into town so he thought he would see how the man was getting on with the prized dog. He asked the man how the dog was and the man replied 'Well, shortly after I took him home I went hunting with a couple of friends so that I could show him off. However, it was a disaster. When we got to a promising looking field, I bent down, lifted the dog's ear up and whispered 'Go find the birds!' The dog immediately ran off at top speed, but he then started barking furiously whilst running about all over the place. The next thing I knew, he had jumped onto my leg and started to hump it as if I was a bitch on heat! After a bit he jumped off my leg, grabbed a stick and stated shaking it at me. I thought that either he had gone mad, or else he had caught rabies so I shot him.'

'You imbecile' the farmer screamed. 'The poor thing was just trying to tell you that there were more f***ing birds out there than you could shake a stick at!'

HOOK, LINE AND SINKER

A man walked into a fishmonger's and asked for six trout.

'Certainly Sir' said the fishmonger. He was just about to start wrapping them up when the man stopped him saying 'I'm sorry but before you do that do you mind throwing the fish to me first?'

'Of course' replied the fishmonger 'but why on earth do you want me to do that?'

'Because I've been fishing all day and I haven't caught a thing. If you throw these trout to me before you wrap them up then I can take them home and honestly say to my wife that I've caught six trout today.

A tourist was fishing off the Sydney coast when his boat capsized. He could swim, but clung on to the side of the upturned boat as he was terrified of the alligators which he'd heard lived off the Australian coast. Seeing a local standing on the beach, the tourist shouted 'Are there any 'gators around here?'

'No' the man replied. 'There haven't been any round these parts for years.'

Feeling reassured, the tourist began to swim back to shore at a leisurely pace and was quite enjoying his unexpected swim. Halfway between the capsized boat and the beach he asked the local 'How did you get rid of the alligators?'

'We didn't have to do anything.' The local replied. 'The sharks soon got rid of them.'

Two neighbours were chatting about their respective husbands. 'I don't want to bring you down' said one, 'but you can't possibly believe your husband when he says that he's been out fishing all night. For one thing, he's never caught a single fish.'

'I know' replied her neighbour 'that's exactly why I do believe him.'

The wife said to her cheating husband 'There was a phone call for you whilst you were out.'

'Who was it from' enquired the husband.

'It was one of those trouts you said you went fishing for last week' came the angry reply.

Paddy was enjoying a quiet day fishing when a game warden approached him. 'Excuse me' the warden said, 'but you need a permit in order to fish here.'

Paddy looked at the huge pile of fish that he had successfully caught and replied in a puzzled voice 'But why? As you can see, I'm doing very well with a worm.'

Bill and Simon were discussing the day they'd just spent fishing. 'To tell you the truth' said Bill, 'the fishing wasn't very good today.'

'But you told me you'd had 30 bites' replied Simon.

'I did' said Bill. 'One small fish and 29 mosquito bites.'

The little boy moaned to his mother 'I'm never going to take my sister fishing with me again.'

'Why ever not?' said the mother. 'I know she's only little, but the water isn't very deep and you can swim so what is the problem?'

'She keeps eating all of my maggots' replied the son.

Claire had been out for the day fishing with four male friends and returned home that evening with a red snapper.

The man was walking down by the river looking for a suitable place to start fishing. He saw a fisherman on the riverbank so he called out to him 'Is this a good river for fish?'
'It certainly is' replied the fisherman 'because they don't seem to want to come out of it.'

Steven thought that he had had a very successful day fly-fishing. He returned home with a blue-bottle, a midge and a pair of trousers.

The real reason that men like fishing is that it's the only time anyone will ever say to them 'Wow! That's a big one!'

I know of a nurse who hates fishing, but she never seems to mind going down on the docks.

Lisa was only a fisherman's daughter, but she knew her plaice and how to fillet.

STUPENDOUSLY SCARY SPORTS

A parachutist who always carried his parachute as hand luggage had checked in for a flight to the USA and was entering the departure lounge. When he reached the X-ray machine the inspector insisted that the parachutist open up his parachute to prove that there was nothing hidden in it. The parachutist tried to avoid this as it would take such a long time to repack it, but after quite an argument he was forced to open his chute, and just managed to get it repacked in time to make his flight.

He sat down in his seat, and was finally beginning to calm down a bit when he overheard the elderly couple next to him talking about him.

The old man said to his wife 'Ethel, that young man just put a parachute under his seat.' The old woman as usual didn't quite believe her husband, so she turned to the parachutist and said, 'Have you really brought a parachute?'

'Yes of course,' replied the still irritated parachutist. 'Were you not given yours?'

What's the difference between a golfer and a parachute jumper?
A golfer goes 'Whack, f**k' and a parachutist goes 'F**k, whack.'

The unfortunate Irish parachutist realised that he had problems when his snorkel wouldn't open.

If at first you don't succeed, then perhaps BASE jumping isn't the sport for you.

BASE jumping is an excellent way to relax. You can really take your mind off your problems.

Why do mountain climbers rope themselves together? In order to stop anyone who accidentally comes to his or her senses from going home.

GOLF AND RELIGION

The two keen golfers frequently argued about whether you could play golf in heaven. Finally they came to the agreement that the first one to die would see if you were able to play golf in heaven or not, and would then come back and tell the other.

Years later on of the golfers died, and shortly afterwards came back to visit his friend. 'I have both good news and bad news' he said. 'The good news is that you can play golf as often as you like in heaven. The bad news is that you are the next up to tee.'

Q: Why did God invent golf?
A: So that men had a reason to get dressed up like pimps.

A builder and a priest were playing golf, but unfortunately the builder wasn't very good at the game, and would say loudly 'F**k, missed!' every time he missed.

After several outbursts of this nature, the

poor priest could take it no longer, and said to the builder 'Do not swear or God will punish you.' However his request made no difference, and the builder continued to swear every time he missed a stroke.

After another few exclamations the priest was getting very angry, and again said to the builder 'I insist that you stop swearing this minute, otherwise God will hear you, and he will punish you.'

Once more it made no difference, and after his next missed shot the builder shouted out 'F**k, missed!' Straight afterwards a bolt of lightning flew out of the sky, hitting the priest and killing him straight away.

Suddenly a voice was heard in the clouds 'F**k, missed!'

A golfer had agreed to a round with the local priest. At the first hole the priest asked 'Which club are you going to use on this hole?'

The golfer answered 'I'm going to use an eight iron, father. What will you be using?'

The priest said 'I'm going to hit a seven and pray.'

The golfer hit his eight iron and the ball landed really close to the green. However when it came to the priests turn, he hit his seven, and the ball ended up only a few yards in front of him.

The golfer turned to the priest and said 'I don't know how it works in your church, father, but in mine we always keep our head down when we pray.'

The golf player had just hit his drive from the first straight into the rough, and it had landed at the bottom of a tree. The golfer was very angry with himself for this, so he hit the ball with considerable force as he attempted to clear it. The ball bounced off the tree, hitting the golfer on the head and killing him.

As he arrived at the Pearly Gates he met St. Peter he said to him 'Well, I see that you were a keen golfer, is that correct?'

'Yes it is' the golfer replied.

St. Peter then asked 'Could you hit the ball a long way?'

'Of course' the golfer replied. 'I got here in two didn't I?'

A vicar had just hit his ball into a bunker. He was obviously very annoyed, but managed to keep his composure, and remained silent. When he got to his ball, he found that it was right in the corner of the bunker, so would be extremely difficult for him to clear without wasting quite a few shots. However, even though he was by now grimacing, he still managed to stay silent, and didn't utter a single word of annoyance at finding himself in this position.

Eventually, having wasted five shots, he managed to free the ball from the bunker, only to watch in dismay as it continued rolling towards a small stream. After seeing his ball splash into the water, he could no longer hide his anger. He grabbed his golf club and snapped it in half, then he threw all of his remaining golf balls into the stream as well and finally he threw his tees into the rough. He then regained control of himself, and quietly said 'It's no good, I'm just going to have to give it up.'

His playing partner said with great sympathy 'That's a pity. I think that you will really miss the game.'

Astonished, the vicar replied 'I'm not giving up golf you idiot. As of this moment I'm giving up the f**king church.'

Fred was a keen golfer, but he was sadly lacking in talent for the game. He would play a round of golf every Saturday at his local club, and always had trouble at the ninth hole. Every week he would hit his golf ball into the rough, and every week he would then be unable to find his golf ball in the rough.

One week he decided that he was fed up of losing all his expensive new golf balls on this hole, so he decided to ball with one of his really old, battered golf balls so that it wouldn't matter so much if he lost it. He placed the old ball on the tee, and was just about to take a swing at the ball, when a voice boomed down from the sky 'Use the new ball.'

Fred decided that the voice from up high must know what it was talking about, so he replaced the old ball, for a new top of the range golf ball, and was just taking a backswing when the voice again spoke. 'Take a practice swing.'

So Fred once again decided to follow the advice he had been given. He stepped away from the tee and practised the shot that he was about to make. Suddenly the voice spoke for the final time. 'Use the old ball.'

The golfer had obviously missed one putt too many, because he was seen throwing down his putter and dropping to his knees. Raising his arms to the heavens he was heard to exclaim 'I can't take it anymore. I demand that you come down here and play me properly. Bring your father if you like, I don't care as long as you fight fair.'

The elderly golfer passed away. When his will was read, it stated that he wished to be buried on the green of the 12th hole on his local golf course, which he had played regularly for 25 years. The 12th hole was a very long hole, with a huge bunker almost directly in front of the small green. In all of his twenty-five years playing the golf course, the elderly golfer had never managed to avoid landing in the bunker. That was the reason why he wanted to rest for eternity on the green.

Unfortunately it was decided that the man couldn't be buried on the green, as it might put people off playing the hole. However, the golf club directors did agree that if he was cremated his ashes could be sprinkled on the green, and in that way he would get his wish.

A week later the man's widow and golfing friends gathered round the 12th hole to sprinkle his ashes. A number of moving speeches were made in tribute to the man before his widow slowly began to pour his ashes over the green.

Suddenly, without warning a huge gust of wind blew from the back of the green and the group watched in despair as the wind carried the ashes, and laid the man to rest for eternity in the bunker.

When Charles turned up for a round of golf on Sunday morning his golfing friends were very surprised. 'What are you doing here?' one of them enquired. 'You don't usually play golf on a Sunday because you go to church with your wife.'

'Well' Charles replied 'it was a toss-up between golf and going to church. I had to toss 12 times.'

The hacker went onto the course for a round of golf and paired up with a priest. As they played the first nine the hacker noticed that before every shot he made, the priest would get down on his hands and knees and pray to the Lord for a successful shot.

After watching the priest hit a spectacular shot the hacker turned to the priest and said 'Father, can I ask you a question?'

'Of course' the priest replied. 'What would you like to know?'

'Well, before every shot you take you kneel down and pray. Why do you do that?'

'I pray before every shot so that I can count on the Lord's assistance to help my ball fly straight and true.'

'That's a great idea' the hacker said. 'Do you think that it would work for me?'

'No, I'm afraid that it wouldn't' the priest replied.

'Why not' asked the surprised hacker.

'Because my son' the priest replied, 'you are such a terrible player.'

Four friends had paired up one afternoon for a round of golf. As they got midway around the course they looked up to the sky to see huge storm clouds gathering overhead. Although the clouds were black, they decided they should just have time to finish their game if they were quick. They decided that they would just have to make sure that they were always ahead of the clouds. As they finished the next hole they heard thunder in the distance and as they finished the next hole the thunder sounded a little bit nearer. They arrived at the next tee, and as soon as the first golfer was about to hit the ball the storm closed in. There was a huge clap of thunder, followed by a bolt of lightning which missed the first golfer by about 20 foot.

'That is it!' he exclaimed, grabbing his golf clubs and rushing off towards the club house. 'I don't care what you lot think, but as far as I'm concerned when God says that he wants to play through, he plays through.'

A man had gone to his local golf club for a quick round of golf, and managed to find someone to pair up with. They teed off and everything went as normal until the fifth hole, when the man noticed that his golfing partner had an odd habit. Every time they got to the green, the golfer would reach into his golf bag and pull out a huge floppy hat. He would then put it on his head until he'd putted the ball into the hole. Then he would take the hat off and put it back into his bag before continuing to the next hole. This odd behaviour continued for the next few holes, until finally, the man was desperate for an explanation.

'I don't mean to appear rude' he began, 'but I have to ask, why do you put on that ridiculous hat before you putt – but take it off as soon as you have finished?'

'I wondered if you would notice' the man explained. 'I have to put the hat on before each time I putt because I am the Lord's worst putter.'

'I'm sorry to hear that' the man replied, 'but what has that got to do with the hat?'
'Well, I just thought that if I put the hat on to putt, then maybe the Lord wouldn't notice me.'

A priest had been paired up with a hacker at the local golf course. After completing a few holes the priest was becoming more and more distressed by the man's appalling behaviour. Not only was he a useless golfer, but after every bad shot he hit he would scream out obscenities at the top of his voice. After putting up with an hour of this behaviour the priest could take no more.

'I have to tell you that this sort of behaviour is totally unnecessary. For example, I played with a man last week who shot a six under par, and not once during the entire round did he so much as raise his voice, let alone utter profanities like you are doing.'

'I'm not surprised' the man snapped back. 'At only six under par what did he have to complain about?'

A couple of friends were playing a round when the weather began to turn. It was obvious that a big storm was heading their way. As they continued to the next hole the first golfer turned to his friend and asked him what he got for the previous hole.

'I got a four' his friend answered.

As soon as he had finished speaking the sky above them darkened, and a bolt of lightning came crashing down from the heavens narrowly missing him.

'Okay, okay' he replied. 'Make it a five.'

Two men paired up at the club for a round of golf. They were pleased to discover that they both played off 18 handicaps so they decided to make the round more competitive by playing for money. However, as they reached the seventh hole the first golfer was getting more than a little annoyed. His partner was playing brilliantly for a supposed 18-handicap player. He was either having the round of his life or else he was hustling the first golfer. This thought infuriated the first player, but he decided to remain calm in case the man was just having a lucky day.

He remained calm until the 13th hole. The 13th was a very long hole, a par five with trees on either side, two bunkers and a water trap. The golfer watched with increasing anger as his partner blasted his ball into the air, avoiding the bunkers and landing neatly on the green about a foot from the hole. He shot a look of pure hatred at his partner, who looked back at him and laughed nervously. 'Gosh' he remarked, 'someone up there must really like me.'

'Yes' the golfer steadily replied, heading towards his partner. 'And you are just about to join him.'

On Sunday morning the priest stood by the 18th hole waiting as the teenage boy finished his round of golf. 'It is a Sunday morning, and you are out here playing golf when you should be in church praising our Lord. What would your father have to say about this?' he sternly admonished.

'I don't know, Father' replied the boy. 'But he's just behind me, so you can ask him yourself.'

The two friends were leaving church on a Sunday morning when they started chatting to each other. 'You know' one said to the other 'I can always tell who plays golf out of the church congregation.'

'How can you tell that?' his friend enquired.

'It's simple' his friend answered. 'I just look to see who prays with an interlocking grip.'

A priest decided to play a round of golf and soon found himself a young man in the clubhouse to play a round with. The priest warned the man that he was new to the game but that he would try not to hold him up too much.

'Don't worry, Father' the youngster replied. 'I'm actually a golf pro. If there is anything that you need to know or if you have any questions about the game please feel free to ask me. I will help you in any way that I can.'

Why thank you' said the priest. 'That would be very much appreciated.'

During the course of the game the priest took advantage of the man's answer and asked him a variety of questions on how to improve his game. When they finished the 18th hole the priest thanked the man for his help and started to walk away.

'Just a minute, Father' the young man said.

'What is it my son?' the priest enquired.

'You owe me £50.'

'Why do I owe you £50?' the priest asked.

'Because before we started playing I told you that I was a golf pro. That is how I make my living and since I have answered all of your questions it is only fair that I get paid for my services.'

'Very well my son' replied the priest, who was very annoyed. 'However, I don't have the money on me at the moment. You will have to come to church tomorrow morning before the service and I'll give you your money.'

'Okay' said the young man walking away, 'I'll see you tomorrow.'

'Don't forget to bring your mother and father with you when you come to the church' the priest called out.

'Why should I bring my mother and father with me?' the young man enquired.

'So that I can marry them for you!' the priest responded.

Ethel and Alf were a lovely old couple who loved each other dearly, and loved nothing more than passing their retirement by playing golf together. They were not particularly well off, but they always managed to scrape together the money to play at their local golf course.

They were both over 80 years old, so it wasn't long before they passed away. In fact they were so in love that they died on the same day, as they couldn't live without one another.

They arrived at the pearly gates to find St. Peter waiting for them. 'As you have been such good and kind people we have decided to reward you for all eternity.'

With that he led them through the pearly gates and up to a beautiful golf course, where a magnificent mansion which overlooked the entire course stood alongside the first hole.
'This is all yours' St. Peter said. 'It is your just reward for your peaceful life.'

Alf just stood there in silence looking at the golf course. 'This is wonderful' Ethel exclaimed. 'Thank you ever so much. Can we play the course immediately?'

'Of course you can' St. Peter said. He led them round to the side of their new home to a golf cart with two new sets of golf clubs inside it. They went off round the course, and by the time they had got to the fourth tee Ethel noticed that her dear Alf hadn't said a single word since St. Peter had shown them their new home. 'Is everything alright darling?' Ethel enquired.

Alf turned round and stared at Ethel. She was horrified to see his face turn bright red with anger (in all of the time that they had been married he hadn't so much as raised his voice at her.) 'Is everything alright?' he shouted. 'For sixty years, all you said to me was 'don't drink, don't smoke, don't eat fatty foods, drive carefully and get enough sleep.' If you had just left me alone I could have been here much earlier.'

DIRTY DANCING

Q: Why do ballerinas wear tights?
A: So that they don't stick to the floor when they do the splits.

Paul was a very shy boy, but had managed to puck up the courage to take a lovely young lady dancing with him. As they danced away he could feel his confidence growing until halfway through the second dance, when the clasp on the girl's necklace broke and it slid down the back of her dress.

'Will you reach down and get it for me?' she asked Paul. His face grew redder and redder as he tried to feel for the necklace, but he couldn't find it.

'Try further down' the girl advised. Realising that everyone was now staring at them, Paul whispered 'I feel a perfect a*se.'

'My tits aren't bad either' his partner loudly replied, 'but stop wasting time and find my necklace.'

The club's new go-go dancer was so bad that the patrons all agreed that she was more like a gone-gone dancer.

Simon had been banned from the hokey-cokey dancing class. He kept putting it in when he should have been shaking it all about.

Two elderly ladies were quietly reminiscing about their old dancing days. 'Do you remember that wonderful evening at the Blackpool?'

'Oh, yes' the second replied. 'That was a wonderful evening. What about the minuet?'

'How do you expect me to remember the men I ate? I can hardly remember the men I f***ed.'

Mabel was explaining to Eileen why she had suddenly had to give up her tap-dancing career. 'The problem was that I kept falling off the taps.'

Suzie the chorus girl could often be heard to remark that her left leg wasn't bad, her right leg was a little better, but that between the two she would make her fortune.

The owner of the club walked into the dance studio to check up on his dancers' progress. 'What's going on?' he asked his choreographer.

The choreographer replied 'What you see now is the chorus girls practising the beautiful 'Dance of the Virgins.''

'That must be difficult for them' the club owner cheekily responded. 'It's not easy to rely on memory.'

A buck rabbit went to a barn dance but was quickly asked to leave. He kept trying to do the dozy doe in the corner.

IT'S A KNOCKOUT

BOXER: A bloke who stands up for other people's rights.

Two heavyweight contenders, Jack Jones and Bob Brown arranged a fight to finally sort out the long running feud over who was the better of the two. Midway through the fifth round, Jones threw a hard right punch that sent Brown flying to the ground and knocked him out for the count. As his entourage helped to carry him from the ring on a stretcher, he managed to whisper, 'What happened? I'm in agony.'

'Don't worry,' replied his manager. 'You're in better shape than Jones.'

'But I don't remember hitting him' protested the dazed boxer.

'You were nowhere near him,' the manager replied. 'But nevertheless he's in a much worse state than you. He thinks he killed you in the ring.'

The elderly gentleman enjoyed boasting of his days as a boxer to his numerous grand children. Describing one fight he said 'The bell for the start of the round sounded and we met in the centre of the ring. First my opponent threw a right cross and then he threw a left cross.'

'What happened next, granddad?' the grandchildren asked.

'Then came the Red Cross' he replied.

After so many husbands, and with her age beginning to show, Elizabeth Taylor decided that it would be a good time to tighten up her vaginal area, not the least because she had a new young beau. She went to an eminent Hollywood plastic surgeon, who had carried out her face lifts, boob jobs and stomach staples. Sworn to secrecy, he promised that no-one but him would ever know about her surgery. The delicate operation took several hours, with the surgeon carefully cutting away the spare flesh.

When Elizabeth awoke the following morning she was horrified to see three get well cards in her room, and demanded to see the doctor.

'You promised me you'd keep it secret! How do you explain the cards?' she asked.

'Well,' replied the surgeon, 'the first card is from my wife and I. We hope you'll be feeling better soon.'

'That's very kind' said Liz, 'but what about the other two?'

'The second is from our hospital cleaner. She's a big fan of yours, and has cleaned up after all your other operations. She can definitely be trusted.'

'What a beautiful thought, from such a humble person – I'm really touched,' replied Liz. 'But that still doesn't explain who the third is from.'

'Oh,' said the doctor, 'That's from Evander Holyfield. He wanted to thank you for his new ear.'

Our story begins at the Olympics where the wrestling event was about to take place. The Russian and the American representatives are due to compete in the final for the gold medal. In the dressing room, the American wrestler's trainer came to him and said, 'Don't forget all of the research we've done on the Russian. He's never lost a match because of this 'figure of eight' hold he has. Whatever happens, you must not let him get you in this hold. If he does you won't stand a chance.'

The wrestler went into the ring thinking about what his trainer had said. The match got underway and the two wrestlers began circling each other looking for their chance to attack. Suddenly the Russian attacked, grapping the American wrestler and wrapping him into the terrible 'figure of eight' hold.

A murmur of disappointment could be heard in the crowd and the trainer feared the worst for his wrestler.

Suddenly there was a terrible scream, and a resounding cheer from the crowd. The trainer looked up just in time to see the Russian champion flying across the ring. The Russian landed on the mat, and the American fighter managed to collapse on top of him, pinning him down and winning the match.

The trainer was amazed. When he got the American wrestler alone he asked 'How on earth did you ever get out of the awful 'figure of eight' hold? No one has ever done it before.'

The American wrestler replied 'Well, I was ready to give up when he got me in that hold, but at the last moment, I opened my eyes and saw this pair of balls right in front of my face. I thought I had nothing to lose, so with my last ounce of strength. I stretched out my neck and bit those babies as hard as I could. You'd be amazed how strong you get when you bite your own balls.'

Boxing is a lot like ballet. Except of course, that there's no music, no choreography, and the dancers punch each other. All-in wrestling however is exactly like ballet.

You know you've been watching too much all-in wrestling when the top of your wardrobe has footprints on it from where you've been jumping off the ropes.

Fred's Aunt Mabel took up wrestling and body-building recently. She did so well at it that now she's Fred's uncle.

Paul the boxer had a deadly rabbit punch. The only problem was that he kept having to fight people.

MORE QUICK QUOTATIONS

'The Queen's Park Oval, exactly as its name suggests – absolutely round.'
Tony Cozier.

'....and Ray Illingworth is relieving himself in front of the pavilion.'
John Arlott.

'Henry Horton's got a funny stance. It looks as if he's shi**ing on a sooting stick.'
Brian Johnston.

'....and later we will have action from the men's cockless pairs.'
Sue Barker.

'I can't tell you who's leading – It's either Oxford or Cambridge.'
John Snagge.

'Ah, isn't that nice, the wife of the Cambridge president is kissing the cox of the Oxford crew.'
Harry Carpenter.

'Morcelli has four fastest 1500-metre times ever. And all those times are at 1500 metres.'
David Coleman.

'Her time is about 4.33, which she's capable of.'
David Coleman.

'There goes Juantorena down the back straight, opening his legs and showing his class.'
David Coleman.

'There is Brendan Foster, by himself, with 20,000 people.'
David Coleman.

'And here's Moses Kiptanui – the 19-year-old Kenyan, who turned 20 a few weeks ago.'
David Coleman.

'Watch the time – it gives you an indication of how fast they are running.'
Ron Pickering.

'And with an alphabetical irony, Nigeria follows New Zealand.'
David Coleman.

'Well, you gave the horse a wonderful ride, everybody saw that.'
Desmond Lynam.

'This is really a lovely horse, I once rode her mother.'
Ted Walsh.

Dennis Pennis: 'Have you ever thought of writing your autobiography?'
Chris Eubank: 'On what?'

'I'll fight Lloyd Honeyghan for nothing if the price is right.'
Marlon Starling.

'Joe Frazier is so ugly he should donate his face to the US Bureau of Wildlife.'
Muhammad Ali.

'A lot of boxing promoters couldn't match the cheeks of their backsides.'
Mickey Duff.

'Eubank is as genuine as a three dollar bill.'
Mickey Duff on Chris Eubank.

'We've been trying to get Elvis. He's been dead long enough.'
Ray Foreman on next opponent for George Foreman.

'He's like washing-up liquid: built on hype and one day the bubble will burst.'
Chris Eubank on Nigel Benn.

'Sure there have been injuries and deaths in boxing – but none of them serious.'
Alan Minter.

'I was in a no-win situation, so I'm glad that I won rather than lost.'
Frank Bruno.

'I owe a lot to my parents, especially my mother and father.'
Greg Norman.

'One of the reasons Arnie (Arnold Palmer) is playing so well is that, before each tee-shot, his wife takes out his balls and kisses them. – Oh my God, what have I just said?'
U.S. TV commentator.

'Golf is a lot of walking, broken up by disappointment and bad arithmetic.'
Mark Twain.

'Golf: a game in which you claim the privileges of age, and retain the playthings of childhood.'
Samuel Johnson.

'Golf is too slow a game for Canada. We would go to sleep over it.'
John B. McLenan.

'I regard golf as an expensive way of playing marbles.'
G. K. Chesterton.

'Golf is a good walk spoiled.'
Mark Twain.

'The only time he opens his mouth is to change feet.'
David Feherty on Nick Faldo.

'He has a face like a warthog that has been stung by a wasp.'
David Feherty on Colin Montgomerie.

'We now have exactly the same position as we had at the start of the race, only exactly the opposite.'
Murray Walker.

'The lead car is absolutely unique, except for the one behind it which is identical.'
Murray Walker.

'Just under 10 seconds for Nigel Mansell. Call it 9.5 seconds in round numbers.'
Murray Walker.

'Someone with about as much charisma as a damp spark plug.'
Alan Hubbard, *Observer*, on Nigel Mansell.

'He is so brave, but such a moaner. He should have 'He Who Dares Whines' embroidered on his overalls.'
Simon Barnes on Nigel Mansell.

'Fred Davis, the doyen of snooker, now 67 years of age and too old to get his leg over, prefers to use his left hand.'
Ted Lowe.

'I'm not into working out. My philosophy: No pain, no pain.'
Carol Leifer.

'Every time I feel the urge to exercise, I lie down until it goes away.'
Mark Twain.

THE RULES OF CRICKET

There are two sides. One is out in the field and one is in.

Each man that is in the side that's in goes out, and when he's out he comes back in. Then the next man goes in (that is out) until he's out, at which point he comes in.

When all of the men in the side that's in are out, the side that is out comes in and the side that has been in goes out, and tries to get those coming in out.

Sometimes you get men still in and not out.

When both sides have been in and out including the not outs, that is the end of the game.

However, if the game is washed out no-one gets to go in, but everyone stays inside and no-one gets out.

The bowling takes place in overs, in which the bowler can hurl the ball as fast as he can at the wicket to get the batsman out, and the batsman who is in tries to hit the ball as hard as he can.

An over lasts six balls, after which the over is over, unless it is Australian when there are two more balls before the over is really over.

Each match takes five days. It takes this long because they need time to figure out who is in i.e. out, and who is out i.e. in, and who is not out, but not yet in.

There are also one-day matches, which oddly enough are often played at night, in which everyone is in a hurry to get in and stay out.

SPORTING U.S.A.

Three baseball fans were on their way to a game when they noticed a foot sticking out of the bushes by the side of the road. They looked into the bushes and found a dead lady who to their surprise was completely naked.

Out of respect for the dead, the three baseball fans couldn't leave her totally naked, so the first man took off his Cubs baseball cap, and put it over her right breast. Next the second man took off his Red Sox baseball cap, and placed it over the lady's left breast. Finally the third man took off his Yankees baseball cap and placed it over the woman's crotch.

They then called the police to report the dead body and when the officer arrived he conducted his inspection of the scene. First, he lifted up the Cubs baseball cap, replaced it and then jotted some notes down in his notebook. Next he lifted up the Red Sox baseball cap, replaced it and then made some more notes in his notebook. The officer then lifted up the Yankees cap, replaced it, lifted it up again, replaced and then lifted it up for a third time before finally replacing it.

The Yankee fan was getting quite upset at the officer's apparent lack of respect for the dead woman, and finally he asked 'What are you, some kind of a pervert? Why do you keep on lifting the cap off the lady's crotch?' The officer replied 'I'm sorry to offend you, but I am simply surprised. You see, normally when I look under a Yankees hat I find an asshole.'

Did you hear about the baseball player with four balls?

He walked to first base.

Stuart was a baseball pitcher with a winning way with women. Unfortunately, his image as a ladies man took a downward turn after he caught a line drive on the fly.

Mr. Jones was thrilled when his daughter Katy phoned from university. However, he was less impressed when she told him that she had been made captain of the softball team.

Why doesn't Mexico have an Olympic team?

Because everybody who can run, jump and swim is already in America.

A woman met a famous American basketball player in a bar. They were getting on very well so the woman agreed to go back to his hotel room with him. He removed his shirt and she saw that he had a tattoo on his arm that read 'Reebok.' She thought that that was a bit strange, so she asked the basketball player why he had the name of a sportswear company tattooed on his arm.

'Well' he replied, 'when I play basketball, my top is sleeveless, so the television cameras show my tattoo, and Reebok pay me for advertising their products.'

After a few minutes, the basketball player took off his trousers, and the woman noticed that he had the word 'Puma' tattooed on his leg. She asked the basketball player about the significance of that tattoo, and he gave the same explanation as he had before.

Finally the basketball player took off his pants, and the woman was horrified to see that he had the word 'AIDS' tattooed on his willy. 'No way am I sleeping with a bloke who has AIDS' she screamed. The basketball player calmly replied 'Don't worry baby, in a minute it will say ADIDAS.'

There is a sport in the Olympic Games where competitors have to track through the deep snow, stop to shoot a gun and then run off. Mostly, it is referred to as the 'biathlon.' However in America it is known as 'winter.'

College Entrance Exam for Student Athletes: Time limit: 3 weeks.

1. Metric conversion. How many feet is 0.0 metres?

2. What language is spoken in Germany?

3. Would you ask William Shakespeare to
   a) build a bridge.
   b) Sail the ocean.
   c) Lead an army.
   d) WRITE A PLAY.

4. Can you explain Einstein's Theory of Relativity?
Yes.   No.

5. What are people in America's far north called?
Westerners. Southerners.   Northerners.

6. Advanced maths. If I have three apples how many apples do I have?

7. Discuss the main themes of *Hamlet*. Or spell your name in block capitals.

8. Six Kings of England have been called George, the last one being George the Sixth. Name the previous five.

9. How many commandments was Moses given? (approximately)

10. Spell Bush; Carter; Clinton.
Bush:
Carter:
Clinton:

FITNESS FUNNIES

Q: What is the difference between an aerobics instructor and a dentist?
A: A dentist lets you sit down while he hurts you.

Q: What's the difference between an aerobics instructor and a well-mannered professional torturer?
A: The torturer would apologize first.

Q: What do you call an aerobics instructor who doesn't cause pain and agony?
A: Unemployed.

Q: Why did the aerobics instructor cross the road?
A: Someone on the other side could still walk.

Q: An ethical lawyer, an honest politician, and a merciful aerobics instructor fall out of an aeroplane. Which one hits the ground first?
A: It doesn't matter – none of them exist.

Q: How many aerobics instructors does it take to change a light bulb?
A: Four!...Three!...Two!...One!

Brian was walking down the street when he passed a fitness centre with a sign in the window which read: 'Lose five pounds in five minutes – £25.'

Brian had a few pounds he wanted to lose, so he went inside as this seemed like quite a good deal. He paid his money at reception and was then shown into a gymnasium. A beautiful young girl entered the gym. She was naked except for a small sign around her waist which read 'If you catch me, this is yours.' On the bottom of the sign there was a large arrow pointing downwards.

Upon seeing this, Brian immediately gave chase. He ran about all over the gym after the girl, but after about five minutes he still hadn't been able to catch her. Stepping on to the scales he was delighted to see that he was five pounds lighter than before.

Leaving the fitness centre Brian carried on walking down the road. He had only gone a short distance when he saw another fitness centre. This one advertised an even more impressive weight loss treatment. The sign read: 'Lose ten pounds in five minutes – £50.' Brian thought that the opportunity to double his weight loss was too good to miss, so he went into the fitness centre and paid the fee. As before he was shown to the gym. However, this time he was greeted by a tall, very muscular man. He was also naked, and like the girl he had a sign around his waist. Only this one read: 'If I catch you, you get this.'

Bob had just finished his run through the park, so he threw himself on to the grass and started to do some push-ups. Just then the village idiot walked past.

'I hate to tell you' the idiot said, 'but I'm afraid that she's slipped away.'

'Joggers are basically neurotic, bony, smug types who could bore the paint off a DC-10. It is a scientifically proven fact that having to sit through a three-minute conversation between two joggers will cause your IQ to drop 13 points.'

Rick Reilly, *Sports Illustrated*.

The man realised that his sexual stamina wasn't what it had been, so he went to his doctor to ask his advice.

'Your muscle tone is bad, and you are out of

shape' the doctor said. 'I suggest that you go jogging five miles a day.'

The man hated all forms of exercise, but he reluctantly agreed as the doctor insisted that this was the only cure for his problem. A week later the man phoned the doctor to let him know how he was progressing.

'How are you feeling now?' the doctor enquired.

'Great' the man replied happily.

'How is your sex life now?' the doctor asked.

'How should I know' the patient responded. 'I'm 35 miles from home.'

The couple were having a lovely time together when the front door opened. 'Quick' the woman said, 'that will be my husband. Jump out of the window.' He jumped straight out of the window, dashed across the park and merged in with a group of joggers.

After he had run for several miles he knew that he had escaped without detection, but the jogger beside him could contain himself no longer.

'Do you always jog in the nude?' he asked.

'Only in summer' the man replied.

'Do you always jog with a condom on?' the jogger enquired.

'Only when it's raining' he replied.

Joe said that he had learnt to swim at an early age. When he was three his parents would row him out to sea in a little boat until they had got about a mile away from the shore. Then he would have to swim back to shore. Joe said that he quite liked the swim, but getting out of the sack was difficult.

Mr. Gisby-Frilbert was keen to show his new girlfriend his mansion. 'Here is one of my swimming pools' he said. 'I keep this swimming pool filled with cold water as some of my friends prefer to swim in cold water.'

'How considerate' Gabrielle remarked.

As they approached the second swimming pool Mr Gisby-Frilbert said 'This pool is filled with warm water for my friends who prefer to swim in warm water.'

'I'm very impressed' Gabrielle said.

'Finally, here is my third pool' said Mr. Gisby-Frilbert.

Gabrielle said with amazement 'But Gissy, darling, this one is empty.'

'Why naturally' he smoothly replied. 'Not all of my friends like to swim.'

Beach inspector: 'Why have you applied for a position as a lifeguard when you can't even swim? You are just wasting my time.'

Job applicant: 'I know. But at seven feet two inches tall I can wade out quite a long way!'

Toby walked over to the pool lifeguard. 'Excuse me, but what is the best way to teach a girl to swim?' he enquired.

Taking Toby to one side, the lifeguard replied: 'The best way is to walk her into the water, and putting one arm tightly around her waist, run your hand up her arm until your hand is even with hers. Then you lightly twine her fingers...'

'Excuse me' Toby interrupted, 'but she is my sister.'

The lifeguard sneered and said 'In that case just throw her in at the deep end.'

The annual university boat race resulted in an exciting finish, but there was a more dramatic moment when a blonde rushed through the crowd and kissed the cox of the winning crew.

Determined to learn to scuba dive, Mr. Crombie spent thousands of pounds on lessons. He then spent thousands more on the best quality diving suit, tank, mask, and all the necessary equipment. Buying a boat and sailing to the Bahamas he felt very proud that he had managed to learn how to scuba dive successfully.

Diving off his boat for the first time he photographed the coral and the fish, and used his special underwater pen and notepad to make notes on everything he saw. He was surprised to see a man swimming several feet below him without any diving equipment on whatsoever.

Outraged, Mr. Crombie swam over to him and wrote on his pad 'I spent over three thousand pounds to learn to scuba dive, and I find you in a pair of swimming trunks. How do you explain it?'

Taking the pad and pen in his hand the stranger quickly wrote down 'You bastard – I'm drowning.'

Finding a beautiful novice swimmer to instruct, Simon walked her around in the pool. After a while however she became curious and asked 'Will I really sink if you pull it out?'

Sitting around the hotel pool, Jack said to George 'I love bathing beauties.'

'Lucky you!' George replied. 'All I ever get to bathe is the dog.'

Fred wasn't a particularly handsome bloke but neither was his friend William. Yet every day when Fred went to the beach he left empty-handed, whereas William left with a different girl each time. Overcome with curiosity, Fred waited for William to arrive one day, and then asked him: 'Every time we go to the beach, you go home with a gorgeous woman while I go home alone. How do you do it?'

'It's easy' William admitted. 'All I do is get a

tight pair of swimming trunks and stuff a cucumber down them. Then I have no trouble pulling the birds.'

Fred thanked William and hurried to the local shops to buy some tight swimming trunks and a cucumber. However after two more days at the beach Fred still hadn't attracted a single girl, while William continued to have no problem finding girls willing to go home with him.

Fred couldn't understand what was going wrong. Frustrated he went over to William and asked what could be wrong.

'The trunks are fine.' William replied. 'But there is one thing.'

'What is it?' Fred asked.

'Tomorrow you should try putting the cucumber down the front of your trunks.'

Q: Why should you never fall in love with a tennis player.
A: Because to them love means nothing.

A man was talking to an attractive blonde in a bar. 'I'm a little stiff from Badminton.'

'I don't care where you come from' she snootily replied.

Is playing tennis courting disaster – or is it a racket?

Badminton: the reason why the lamb tasted off.

'I wanted to have a career in sports when I was young, but I had to give it up. I'm only six feet tall, so I couldn't play basketball. I'm only 190 pounds, so I couldn't play football. And I have 20-20 vision, so I couldn't be a referee.'
Jay Leno.

'Exercise is bunk. If you are healthy, you don't need it; if you are sick, you shouldn't take it.'
    Henry Ford.

OTHER BOOKS IN THE SERIES:

DANGEROUSLY DARING DIRTY JOKES

SERIOUSLY SICK DRINKING JOKES

THE ABSOLUTELY FRIGHTFUL JOKE BOOK

THE REALLY WICKED JOKE BOOK

THE TRULY TERRIBLE JOKE BOOK